I0693785

CLASS BRITANNIA

Britain, Class and the

Control Model of Society

Alfie Cooke

KATALI EDITIONS

Class Britannia: Britain, Class and the Control Model of Society

Alfie Cooke © 2024
First Published 2024 by Katali Editions, Gravesend, Kent, England

Printed by Amazon

British Library Cataloguing in Publication Data

A catalogue record for this book is available from the British Library

CLASS BRITANNIA

Britain, Class and the Control Model of Society

This book is dedicated to

Linda, Bill and Peter

Scott

and Jesse

Contents

CLASS:

Myths & Legends

Introduction

Class has been pinned on anything and everything: our jobs, our income, and our homes; our education, the accent that we speak with, the manners we display and the way we hold a knife and fork; our hopes and dreams, the television programmes we watch, the sports we follow… A list could drag on endlessly, to include every aspect of our existence down to the minutest detail. We could create precise questionnaires, analyse and summarise our findings, recording the results in weighty tomes in order to present the perfect picture of class in our society whereby everyone is definitively placed and packaged and neatly labeled and categorised. And it would in all probability be wrong. The reason for this is that the more we try to focus on the tiny details of a person's daily life, the less we see of the over-riding drivers, the impact that they have and how they cause a person to live a particular existence. So, for example, we will look at whether someone 'owns' their own home without ever stopping to consider whether they actually own the bricks and mortar and the land that it sits on, or whether they just own an enormous debt that is attributed to these things in the form of mortgages and loans.

Of all the issues that arise when we consider class, one of the most problematic has been the level of breakdown that we seek to create when dividing up society. The most common fault has been to seek a way to present a greater number of class sets that will encompass every possible division and delineation between one person and the next, often to the point where the concept of class becomes meaningless. Recent models have sought, for example, to place university students into separate class strata according to their choice of course, their family background, their low economic status and their future aspirations for employment. We have also had lower and upper brackets attached to the existing nomenclature of class, the resurfacing of outmoded descriptors from bygone centuries and new branches of terminology conjured to explain away any similarities that might exist between one person and another. Such creations are a smokescreen disguising the true purpose of class division within a society.

While many of these divisions have failed to capture the public imagination, our culture has fully embraced the on-going triptych of the working-, middle- and ruling- or upper-classes. This three-band division – handy, pocket-sized and easily stereotyped – is, of course, as misleading and confusing as a definition could possibly get, not least of all because, while the top and the bottom do at least give us some indication of how we can identify those within them, in between we have perhaps the vaguest identifier possible, encompassing everyone who falls somewhere between one extreme and the other. Over the years, we have been fed particular stereotypes of what this "middle class" would look like, most often through sit-coms on the TV: in the seventies we had *The Good Life* and *Happy Ever After*; in the eighties we had *Terry and June* and *Ever Decreasing Circles* and the possibly most brilliantly through Patricia Routledge's portrayal of "Hyacinth Bucket" in *Keeping Up Appearances* complete with her vest-wearing, Working Class brother-in-Law. But while they may have told us how we should spot this "middle class" – well-spoken, chintz décor, middle-management jobs and pretensions of grandeur – those qualities have nothing to do with social class and are more of an indication of the writers' social prejudices than anything else, always being more about snob-humour than anything that would make sense in terms of a class structure. The historical baggage with which we have loaded each of these terms, the social changes that have passed them by, and our own personal re-shaping of their meaning, all conspire to create a concept of class that tells us little or nothing about our own place in society or that of anyone else.

Then there is the problem caused by the assumption that all classes are in some way connected through a tier of mobility where movement in either direction is an everyday reality, simply because they all happen to occur within a particular society. The language we use –

social ladders, top and bottom, upper and lower – all suggest a hierarchy of one class stacked upon another, and with no obvious barriers between them (and with some blurring of the lines between due to the vagaries of meaning and interpretation) comes the idea that someone can move easily between one level and the next. This, we need to understand, is a nonsense, and suggestions of free and open class mobility are a myth to distract from the reality of existence in modern Britain.

1.1 The Myth Of The Class Ladder

In standard views of society and class systems, we are taught to see it always in terms of hierarchical layers, with the lower levels of society at the bottom and the higher, quite naturally, sitting on top, with all of the classes connected. This is the traditional image that gives us the concept of social class as a ladder - one which, given the right combination of drive, ability and perhaps just a little luck (which of course you can always make yourself!) can be climbed from the very bottom to the very top by anyone of us. This is one of the biggest misunderstandings of class systems in western post-industrial societies, a myth that needs to be dispelled right from the start. Capitalist cultures like to present us with many examples of the 'working-class-lad-becomes-millionaire' scenario and the 'girl-next-door-marries-prince' fantasy and we are filled with stories of the entrepreneur who began with just a barrow in the market and now holds court in the House of Lords. These are only ever exceptions, a rare few cases when we consider the size of our societies and the fact that the overwhelming majority of people work as hard as they can and yet still die with nothing to their name.

So why do we have such exceptions? There must always be exceptions for the system to be maintained. But for every football star who makes it to the big time and earns their fortune, a thousand more will have given up on their dreams even before having left school; for every successful entrepreneur, there will be a thousand more falling into bankruptcy and a lifetime of debt; and for every "common girl" who marries into royalty, a million more will become single mothers facing a life of struggle and poverty[1]. The ladder is not there to be climbed; the ladder is there to give the illusion that there is something which *can* be climbed. The exceptions, rather than proving the former, substantiate the latter.

Ever since the dawn of political theorizing, we have been lead to believe in this hierarchical system, with its

---

[1] The usual examples given of these are Lady Diana Spencer and Kate Middleton, neither of whom could ever really be considered to have come from the Working Class and certainly not what would be considered to be a 'common' background.

clearly marked divisions between one section of society and the next, and the miracle of the simple 'ladder', all its parts interlocking to form a single whole (see Fig. 1). However, even a cursory look at British history shows that there is not simply a delineation marker between the different classes but rather a complete separation between certain sections where transition is effectively impossible.

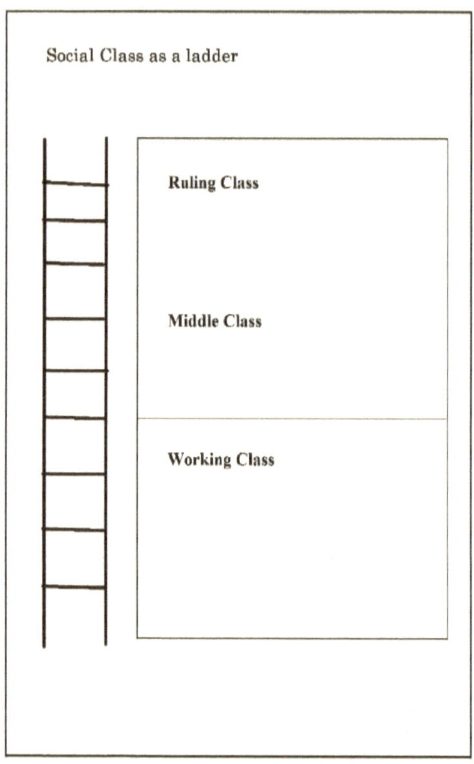

Fig. 1: The Mythical Class Ladder

The 'ladder' concept of class has always been a myth. While there may have been ladders within separate class segments, there has never been a single means by which a person can climb from the bottom end of the Working Class all the way up to the upper-most echelons of the ruling class at the top. The evidence for this can be seen in two of the biggest periods of social upheaval within Britain - the Roman and Norman invasions. In both, those working in the fields, baking the bread and tending the animals carried on much as they had before. While some of them may have traded-in their saws for swords, finding new employment to meet the military needs and demands of their new rulers or dying to forestall their takeover, they still formed what was effectively the Working Class of the time. Similarly, those in trades and professions which gave them a special status in society due to their particular skills as workers (what today might be mislabeled as a 'middle' class) remained much as they were before. The only real change came within the group identified as the 'ruling class', where those that were in power either agreed to a new subservience, were replaced by those who were willing to do so, or were replaced by those who had invaded.

During the Roman period, the invaders had already developed a process of assimilation in the other lands they invaded whereby local leaders were allowed to retain much of their power and to continue much as before, as long as they subjugated themselves to the "glory of Rome". While this was something of a drop in status, at a local level their position in society didn't really change, and no one moved up the class ranks to usurp them who wasn't already a part of their existing inner circle. If they agreed to go along with everything their Roman overlords demanded, they wouldn't be subjected to the indignation of enjoying the simple life as one of the workers or worse[2].

Similarly, with the Norman invasion, local barons were utilised wherever possible to maintain the day-to-day running of their lands because the invaders initially lacked the resources and force of numbers to ensure complete control through strength alone. Local leaders wishing to side with the invaders became an invaluable resource, already having the systems in place by which they could continue to implement control. Once this control had been established, the Norman invaders ensured total dominance by removing the local leaders, replacing them with their own barons who would always be loyal. By 1087, only two local leaders remained in position.

---

[2] It should be noted that one of the few recorded instances of Roman rulers trying to completely strip a local ruler of their position and entitlement nearly resulted in them losing complete control of the whole country in the ensuing revolt led by Boudicca.

It is in these two examples that we get an early indication of what social class in Britain is really all about: control. However ill-trained, under-fed and badly armed the lower strata of society are, their overwhelming strength of numbers holds the possibility of them becoming an unstoppable force. As a consequence, it is necessary for those at the top of society to use whatever tools may be available to them to maintain order and ensure control, key amongst these tools being the class system itself and the acceptance of one's place in society.

Perhaps the clearest historical indication of the failure of the 'class ladder' to deliver on its promise came with the end of the English Civil War. With the ultimate demonstration of power in society - the divine rule of kings - brought to an absolute end, we don't see a dramatic shift within the class system but instead just a change from a dictatorship by the monarchy to a dictatorship by an already existing elite. The poor stayed poor, while those in power - with a few notable exceptions - retained their positions. Those with the military might to effectively challenge the status quo, Cromwell's own New Model Army, were packed off to Ireland to unleash misery and violence on the Irish, thereby keeping them busy and out of the government's way.

If a more modern example of the limitations of the ladder analogy of class is required, then we can look at class movement in the nursing profession in the 21st Century. If we look at the career progression of a nurse, we can begin with the lowest rung within the profession, that of the Healthcare Assistant. As the bottom rung on the class ladder within the nursing profession, we are told that, according to the myth, they can improve their position through hard work. This is, of course, a fallacy since their only means to improve their salary or their position beyond the limitations of an annual "cost of living" rise, is to either complete further training or change profession completely. Hard work alone is not going to improve their lot in life.

So, through retraining, our nurse moves up to the next rung on the nursing ladder. But while they may have moved up in terms of their role, they still sit comfortably within the Working Class. Should they wish to climb their career ladder further, they can of course keep retraining but however far they move up in their profession as a nurse, they still remain within the Working Class, even within the role of Senior Sister on a ward. They may be able to move from a rental apartment to a house, have better holidays, drive a newer car, but all of this control over their existence still comes as a direct result of their labour, one of the defining features of the Working Class and they are as far from the top of the class ladder as they always were.

In order to gain greater control, they would need to move into management, effectively changing their career entirely and no longer being a nurse. By gradually working their way up through the ranks, constantly retraining, changing the direction of their career from being a carer to managing carers, and avoiding the pitfalls that arise from daring to have any kind of career break, our 'nurse' is now in a position where they can exercise some element of control over the lives of other people. This may seem to be a significant possibility for climbing the ladder, but when we consider that our nurse may be one of a hundred or more nurses who would be equally suitable for such a management role at any given time, only one of them can make this transition.

After that, there is no further opportunity for anything that would pass for rapid movement. It becomes a "dead man's shoes" situation, with progression only being possible if the post above them is vacated, regardless of the amount of hard work that they put in. Such effort is used by employers to maintain a situation of people giving more and more of themselves in the hope that, one day, this may pay dividends and lead to a promotion or a decent pay rise. In addition, we must also consider the numerous barriers and prejudices in place and the possibility that, since their face might not fit, somebody else has already being *given* the promotion before our nurse was even aware that the post had become available. At this point, it is, perhaps, the right time to reintroduce the key concept of the myth of the class ladder: that anyone can climb it. By reviewing the way we emphasise those few words, we can see what the reality of that 'ladder' actually is: any ONE can climb it, one and only one.

1.2 The Myth of Democracy

In the modern democracy, we are lead to believe that such forms of government empower us all, giving control to everyone: Every adult has the freedom to exercise their right to vote, with the power to hold their political representatives to account. Effectively, each of them has been granted an element of control over the decisions being made by a government, and if we don't like what we get, we simply bring in a new one at the next election. Such forms of representative democracy, we are told, give everyone a stake in the management of society. This, however, is a deliberately false presentation of the mechanisms by which the modern democracy functions. What is key is that we *believe* that we have a stake in the management of society, even if such a belief is entirely unfounded.

If we begin by considering our ability to enact major social change by voting in a representative democracy such as that used in Britain, we can see that while we may wish to change the model of government that is used, the system does not allow for such a change to be made. For example, if we take a seemingly straightforward change such as a switch from "first pass the post" to "proportional representation", what is required is for a set of complex conditions to come together at the same time. As a bare minimum, this would be that:

    (1) either of the main parties most likely to win an election adopts it as policy;

    (2) that this party wins enough seats across the whole country to form a government and pass new laws;

    (3) that such a change is prioritised by the new government and doesn't turn out to be just another pre-election promise;

    (4) that this government holds on to power long enough to enact such changes; and

    (5) no subsequent governments change the system back to the previous format.

But even this list is not complete. We could add to this the duplicitous nature of many of those in political office, where they will announce support for a policy as a means to get themselves into a position of power but will then change this immediately they have gained such a position. Then there is the issue that any proposed policies not only require the support of elected politicians for them to come into being, but also the full support of the many civil servants who would be involved at various levels in the creation and passing of a new law, and in addition the support of an unelected House of Lords, who may choose to block policies that may threaten their own position.

The British political system allows for people to be elected to government from one of the widest spectrums of political viewpoints in the Western world. With the anarchists as possibly the only exception, nearly all political viewpoints have been elected to parliament at some point and at every election you will find seats being contested by everyone from the far-left through to the far-right, ecologists through to industrialists and the 'serious' political candidates through to the comic. However, in the past 100 years, politics has been entirely dominated by just three parties: the Conservatives, Labour and the various incarnations of the Liberals. No other political party has ever been represented at national government level, regardless of the number of seats they may have won, and, as a consequence, what we have is an effectively reduced palate from which to choose our next government. What we are told is that the reason there has never been, for example, a communist government in Britain is that the voting public have never chosen to elect such a government. We do, after all, have the right to vote as we please.

However, if we look at the system by which we are given the choices of who we can vote for, we can see immediately that there are specific reasons why such potential representatives would struggle to gain enough seats to be able to form a government. Firstly, we have the problem that our parliaments have been dominated by those same three parties who, in general, secure the bulk of the votes in each constituency. What this means is that, if a government is deeply unpopular, individual members of the electorate see that they have a bleak choice to either vote for their preferred candidate and be unlikely to have any representation, or vote for the one most likely to unseat the government's candidate just to rid themselves of a government they dislike. What this means is that, unless a new candidate fully captures the public's imagination, they are unlikely to succeed. This also needs to happen across the whole of the country to put such a candidate in a position in a government where they would be able to effectively create any lasting change.

Secondly, there is the problem of finances. Standing as a potential candidate isn't free and, if someone does not get enough votes, they will lose their deposit, that is, the money that they put forward to stand as a potential candidate is kept by the state. This means that many people from poorer backgrounds will be discouraged from standing for government unless they can secure the finanicial support of an existing party. In addition, there is the cost of election materials - posters, leaflets etc - where the main political parties have spent years developing methods of funding for their campaigns, including, for example, the ability to arrange cheaper deals with printers so that they can obtain more materials for the same price.

Then, we come to the problem of the dissemination of ideas to which voters have access to. For most of us, what we know about politics comes from the media we consume. In Britain, most newspapers could be classed as being 'establishment', that is, they express views that are in favour of the status quo and are generally right-wing in the views that they express. There are a handful of what are described as the 'left-wing' press but for the most part these are only left-wing when compared to the views expressed in the right-wing media. Essentially, there is only one left-wing daily newspaper available - the *Morning Star* - and many shops do not stock it. Similarly, our television media can be split between the right-wing news outlets (BBC, Sky, ITV, Channel 5) and the liberal outlets (Channel 4). All of these media outlets carry a bias towards the established systems. Many of the new 'freeview' stations do not carry news content and those that do tend to restrict this to celebrity gossip. With such a narrow range of options, many people are only aware of any wider political ideas through word of mouth, and if no one is there to convey the new ideas, they are unlikely to cast a vote in favour of such a candidate.

What this demonstrates is that, while we may have the right and the freedom to vote as we please, our vote is only of consequence where it contributes to the successful election of a particular government. If we happen to have voted for anyone that fails to gain a seat in parliament, our views are no longer represented at all. If the candidate that we chose to vote for gets elected but is not part of the party forming a government, while they may represent our views, they may be unable to effect change in any meaningful way. And even if our elected official is part of the party that forms a government, we are reliant on the views that they expressed to gain our vote being accepted across that party and being part of the policies put forward by the government.

Our freedom to vote is only of any consequence if each vote that is cast results in the voter's view being represented - something that cannot be achieved within the current electoral system. It also requires the voter to have full, unbiased access to the complete range of political perspectives so that informed choices can be made and that our media operate in a politically unbiased way. And this is before we stop to consider the various mechanisms by which political parties may seek to manipulate voters with misinformation, use methods that really should be considered illegal and - for sitting governments - use the standard method of the tax-cut bribe to muster support.

Instead of facilitating our control within society, the modern democratic system allows for control to be maintained within a demographically small coterie of elected officials, senior civil servants, business leaders and royalty, who ensure that they – and those with access to them – maintain their control over the key aspects of society: the system of government; economic policies; legal frameworks etc. The political establishment, reduced to a handful of ideological viewpoints, offers only variations on the same themes. The media presents a similarly limited version of events and a similarly limited set of political options. Without the necessary information to make informed choices, without the political clout as individuals to instigate the dramatic social changes that we may want, the vast majority of people have been rendered powerless, unable to control anything other than the bare basics of their lives.

1.3 The Myth of the Middle Class

Just like the 'class ladder', the existence of a modern 'middle class' is a myth, grown out of a need to establish greater control over those at the blunt end of society's wealth distribution. To be 'middle class' has become synonymous with pretentions of something better: homes in leafy suburbs, jobs in middle management, a university education[3]. The key driver in this generalization of the idea that such a thing as a 'middle class' exists was the indicator of home ownership. As private ownership of living accommodation expanded with the growth of mortgage availability during the 1970s and the creation of the 'right-to-buy' scheme in the following decade so, it was claimed, the middle classes were growing, and that this prosperity had enabled millions of people to escape the misery that was the undoubted lot of their previous existence. Now that they owned something, they had joined the property-owning classes, becoming themselves the "landed gentry" of bygone centuries, escaping the eternal stigma of being that most dreaded of things: working class. The fact that they didn't actually own their home – as many

---

[3] Attending university, as opposed to polytechnic, was once a sign of class superiority, of being 'upper middle class' as opposed to 'lower middle class', with those without such an education being from the 'lower classes'.

discovered when houses began to be repossessed - and were now deep in debt to a mortgage company, without the safety next of social housing, and still obliged to work for everything they had, was neither here nor there – their lives had miraculously changed.

All of this is essentially a means by which to obscure our view of how society actually functions. The way this works is through political sleight of hand, distracting attention from one thing that we should be noticing by making something else seem so much more important. So we are conditioned to miss the massive debts, the lack of any societal support should things go wrong and the lack of any substantial change in our condition, and instead see only the *idea* that we have moved up a rung on the mythical class ladder. Such are the machinations of the class system in Britain: ensure division, distract from unity and facilitate a continuation of the class system in its current form by convincing people that they are something other than what their reality portrays. Effectively, what has been achieved is that a substantial section of the Working Class has been convinced that they are something else, and also that those who still see themselves as Working Class have become convinced that the others have indeed changed, becoming something to be admired and despised in equal turns.

By structuring class systems into such divisions, what social commentators have done is to add credence to the notion that it was better to be in one class than to be in another, not because of any determinable benefits that might be accrued but because the concept of a 'better class' feeds into the concept of a 'better class of people'. Not only would your class be better but, as a consequence, you will become better as a person. Somehow, being deep in a debt that would take a lifetime or more to repay had imbued people with greater personal qualities. And so the divisions between individuals continued: ownership was better than renting; ownership of non-council was better than ownership of ex-council; offices better than building sites; clerical better than manual. Across all aspects of modern life, comparisons were being drawn to provide measures by which the Working Class could alienate themselves from one another. Such is the role of class division that lies at the heart of this myth. What we have come to know as 'middle class' is essentially a means by which to alienate people from the nature of their condition and their role within society and from those others that also share that same endless routine of working to ensure survival.

1.4 The Myth of the Aspirational Class

In some recent forms of class theory, there has been a surge in claims that an individual's aspirations could be used to define the nature of their social class. This began with the notion that those who worked for a living could be separated in to a middle- and a lower- class based upon what they aspired to in life. For example, the 1980s saw an attempt to draw a distinction between those members of the Working Class who merely *sought* to own their own homes and those who considered rented accommodation (including social housing) to be the preferred option. Essentially, both groups aspired to the same thing: to have a place to call home. However, the aforementioned drive to convince everyone that private ownership was better resulted in a form of social engineering by which the precarious nature of mortgage debt – as opposed to the security of easily-affordable, council-owned housing - could lift them out of the Working Class. Yet they still worked to provide themselves with a living, still had minimal control over the means of their existence and, in many cases, found that they had far less control over their housing. But by virtue of *aspiring* for something better they had moved up in the class system and that just by virtue of *wanting* to own their own home, had somehow miraculously altered their place in society. It should be quite clear that using such measures as 'aspiration' as a means by which class can be defined are a nonsense: almost every person who has ever worked has aspired to work less and earn more; almost every parent has aspired to have a better standard of living for their children than they had experienced; almost every revolutionary has aspired to have their own fair share of control. None of this aspiration has changed the nature of the class to which they belong. It just means that, like the rest of us, they have dreamed of something better.

In the wake of the 'greed is good' culture that took hold during the 1980s, it was assumed that class could be separated into those die-hard, retrograde fanatics who clung desperately to the crumbling edifice of their class-consciousness and those who were eager to break free from the shackles of poverty – both financial and spiritual – that came to be understood as the defining features of what we were told was what it meant to be 'working class', so that they could make the entrepreneurial leap into the great promised land of prosperity. The lie that such versions of class gave was that those who work for their living are not a unified entity but rather a disparate collection of feuding factions, each member urged into a partisan hostility towards those not like themselves (or not like their idea of themselves) regardless of the overwhelming similarities they have. This manipulation of society facilitated a continued partition into contending groups, each driven to fight and fend off the others: A social "survival of the fittest" whereby people who are similarly placed in society fight amongst themselves rather than against those who control their existence.

When we look at how society functions, we see that in those classes identified as being in the lower half of society, there is little to distinguish those at the bottom from those at the top. In what we previously saw as the working- and middle classes, we see the same struggle to maintain a decent way of life; we see the same aspirations to provide a better lifestyle for their families, the same need to improve. It may be possible to see differences in the size of their accommodation, the length of their holidays, the age of their car etc., but each of them is caught in a constant cycle of endless toil – or endless unemployment – as they struggle to make ends meet, to pay the rent, to pay the mortgage – in short, to achieve the impossible, to overcome the forces that control their existence. So there is no "aspirational class" where we define people according to their goals in life. Our goals, in essence, are the same: to survive and to have something better, whether that is just for ourselves, our families, or for everyone in society.

1.5 The Division of the Working Class

Throughout the development of class theory, there has been a continued attempt to move away from the basic 3-rung 'ladder' of upper-, middle- and lower- classes and to introduce more intricate layers, as if to show that by increasing the rungs on this mythical class ladder, it is possible to create the appearance of smaller and smaller subdivisions, making it so much easier to climb up to the top. While the initial attempt at defining society had its faults, the diversification and proliferation of class definitions has done nothing to improve on this basic model: it doesn't matter how many subdivisions that the Working Class is carved into, nothing has materially changed in the lives of those being subdivided. Rather, what has happened is that the nature of class has become diluted, watered-down to the point where our understanding of our own place in society has become frail and feint. The purpose of this fragmentation of class becomes so much clearer when we understand class in terms of systems of social control – more of that 1% and their precarious grip on wealth later.

The principle of 'divide and conquer' has long been understood for its military uses but the concept also has political applications whereby control can be maintained by a small social elite over a large population by exploiting whatever divisions exist between different groups within that population and preventing the possibility of them unifying against those in control, who would otherwise be seen as a common enemy. In the political arena of those societies where the wealth of the few greatly out-weighs that of the many, it is important to ensure the existence of perceived divisions within those classes that do not have access to wealth, power or influence in order to prevent this group from becoming disenchanted with the structure of society and rebelling. The first step in this process is the creation of divisions based on working/earning conditions, with the final stages tending to reflect far more aggressive divisions based on ethnicity, religion or culture.

In the first step, the means of division are simple: Split those without access to wealth, power and influence according to their income or the type of job they perform. Thus we have the formation of concepts such as 'blue collar' and 'white collar' jobs. So the team leader, in their store-altered suit, ranks higher than the clerk in their off-the-peg suit, and both sit above the mechanic, in their oil-stained overalls, who in turn sits above the refuse collector. As such, those mechanics, their overalls covered in oil-stains and their heads beneath car bonnets all day find themselves 'relegated' to the 'lower working class', while office workers – generally working in cleaner environments – can be moved up the mythical class ladder to join the 'upper working class'.

Key class definitions from the past have tended to focus on minor financial/aspirational differences in the personal life such as home-ownership, salaries (calculating income weekly versus monthly became important at one point) and work-type differences. While they may still be obliged to work for a living, members of the Working Class are lead to view themselves as having progressed up the 'class ladder' if they have even the smallest promotion. As such, in order to refine their self-definition, they look to see what new bracket of class they fall into, now that they are 'no longer' Working Class. The use of 'middle class', with all its preconceptions of self-improvement and respectability and without any real, clear definition that may interfere with the politically-generated vagaries, works extremely efficiently, with people quickly forgetting that they still have limited control over their lives – their income is only fractionally higher and most of it is still spent on ensuring that they keep a roof over their heads.

This group, however, begins to *believe* that their situation has materially changed and, seeing themselves as more affluent, naturally seeks to separate themselves from other lesser-paid workers. Their aspirations for a better life for themselves and their families have not changed and they may be paying as much on a mortgage as the mechanic pays in rent but they begin to regard themselves as different. Once this happens, they no longer feel any true solidarity with other people who, like them, *work* for a living. Essentially, they no longer see themselves as Working Class because their clothes are cleaner at the end of the day, and similarly they demonstrate no sense of solidarity with anyone other than those who control society.

Separating working people out from the Working Class without them having any distinct improvement over the control they have over their existence and placing them – or convincing them to place themselves - in an entirely fictitious middle class – or into a higher bracket of working class – has the additional effect of creating within them a sense of allegiance with the Controlling Class. They will either see this move as something that they have been *allowed* to do by those in positions of power, through the good graces of their wise decision making, or they will see it as something which they have worked for, in the same way those who rule over them claim to have *worked* for their wealth. Politicians will deliberately garner a 'one-of-the-people' image – visiting factories, supping a pint of beer in a pub – in order to capture this sense that those beneath them can also make that fantastic leap into the world of the rich and powerful.

This myth of the existence of a middle class, some vague grouping that sits somewhere between those who work to live and those who are able to control the lives of those workers, has become the most effective cause of division between members of the Working Class and the difficulty in defining where the Working Class ends and the middle *class* begins is entirely intentional. It allows for the greatest degree of flexibility in providing people with the idea that their aspirational gains have been met without actually providing them with any form of substantial material change in their condition. By utilizing people's own desire for improvement in their own life and that of their families, it is possible to get them to take a different view of themselves. It is no longer necessary to provide evidence that life has got better. If people think that they have moved up a rung on the social ladder, they will ensure that they convince themselves of their change in circumstances. So, despite the fact that they still work for a living, that they do not actually own the home they live in but will be paying off a mortgage (instead of rent) for the rest of their working lives, that they have no change in the amount of control they have over their lives, that the financial gap between them and those who control them is so huge that it is invariably insurmountable and can only be barely comprehended, so they will refuse to admit to their Working Class status, clinging instead to the myth of the *middle class.*

THE CONTROL MODEL OF SOCIETY

Introduction

Whether we choose to accept it or not, our lives are controlled by the systems under which we live. There will be many who will baulk at such as idea, believing themselves to be either free-living spirits who live as they please or neo-liberal conservatives doing away with the interference of government so that everyone is able to live as they please[4]. But whether fuelled by the illusion that you can live outside of the will of society with just a handful of store-bought tools and the (sweat-shop manufactured) clothes on your back, or by the idea that the imposition of state control and state support has created anything other than massive inequality doesn't really matter. Just because you refuse to admit that the earth rotates in an orbit around the sun, doesn't mean that it isn't happening.

In order to begin to understand class division within society, we must first understand the key elements of power by which the life of any person can be controlled and to what extent their ability to maintain full control over their existence is restricted by their access, or lack thereof, to what will be identified as the five Circles of Control. Of course, in an ideal society, everyone would

---

[4] Generally, what the latter group mean by this is the desire to remove those social constraints that prevent them from exercising the type of control that they *want* to wield over others in society.

have equal access to these Circles of Control, so that even those who are entirely dependent on others and/or society as a whole to survive would be able to participate in the decision-making processes to the fullest extent that they are capable. But such societies rarely exist in anything other than our dreams.

What we need to consider is whether the mechanisms by which society functions are used to limit a person's ability to have meaningful control within each of the Circles of Control. Even our democracies, far from being an opportunity for us to exercise our right to chose who does the controlling, are managed in such a way that a change in the system by which governments control us becomes effectively impossible.

There are five different areas of control that an Individual[5] may be able to exercise over their existence. While they are broad in range, it is necessary to avoid attempting to fragment them into smaller divisions as such an activity only degrades our understanding of how both society and class function. These Circles of Control extend in a natural sequence from that which can be held (or not) by an Individual, from the inability to take important decisions over one's own existence, through to the ability to extend control over small groups and on to being able to control society as a whole. These levels of

---

[5] The 'Individual' may comprise of a single person or an inter-dependent group of Individuals such as a family unit.

control can then be used as a framework by which to determine the class structure of a society, by analysing whether such Circles of Control can be accessed by the Individual. The final Circle of Control exists beyond the scope of a society and relates to the impact that other societies or global organisations can have upon it.

2.1 The Circles of Control

Within any functioning society, from the simplest hunter-gather tribes to entire empires, we can identify five potential areas of power that the Individual may have access to:

- Dependent
- Personal
- Communal
- Societal
- Global

The Circles of Control relate directly to these possible forms of power and while they can be used to determine the class structures of such societies, the various circles do not necessary correspond to different social classes as this requires an understanding of the way that access to these Circles of Control is managed and distributed within any given society.

For the Individual, these circles would begin at the stage of dependence on others, where an Individual holds no, or very limited, control over their own existence. This would then be extended through the ability to control elements of their personal existence, through to the Communal and Societal levels where the Individual can exercise power over others and finally ending at global control where control can be exercised over other societies, nations or empires. While the Circle of Global Control exists beyond the scope of societal class structures, it needs to be identified as it has the capacity to impact on all of the other levels of control within a society. For example, while a country may decide to instigate collective ownership of all properties and introduce measures to allow full participation in Societal Control to all their members, impositions by other, larger nations can adversely affect such decisions and prevent any attempt by the people of that first society to do so, such as happened in Chile in 1973 when the USA used its wealth and influence to instigate a military coup against the democratically elected government. Another example of this would be the ongoing blockade of Cuba by, again, the United States.

In Fig. 2, the Circles of Control are presented as concentric to demonstrate that, in most modern societies, each circle contains those that are held within the outer-most Circle of Control. For example, an Individual that

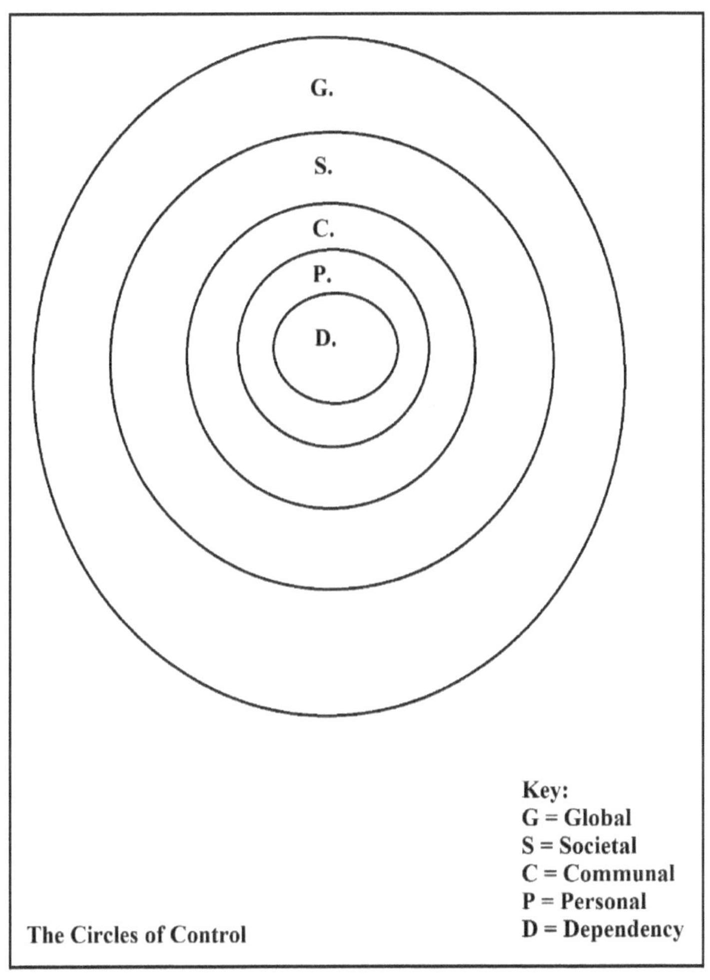

Fig. 2: The Circles of Control

is able to wield power at a Communal level would commonly be able to wield Personal Control over their own existence and to have moved, therefore, beyond the category of dependency. It *is* possible to hold Communal or Societal Control without holding Personal Control but this is a rare occurrence in modern societies.

2.2 The Circles of Control and the Individual

In order to make sense of the systems that we see in any society, it is necessary to view them first in terms of the Circles of Control. To begin with, we must model the society using these Circles of Control and then look at the way in which the Individuals that occupy these Circles of Control relate to those in the others. When we apply the Circles of Control in relation to any given society, we must look at whether an Individual or Individual Unit has any direct access to control their existence or that of others within any given Circle. The first Circles of Control, the Dependent and the Personal, indicate to what extent the Individual holds the power to make those basic decisions over their own existence. For example, this can relate to choices about where they live, where they work, or how their income is spent. The three remaining Circles of Control indicate the Individual's ability to exercise control on a broader level, that is, to extend their controlling influence in order to impact on the existence of others outside of their own Individual Unit within society.

2.2.1 Dependency

The Dependent Circle of Control identifies those situations where an Individual is unable to exercise control over their own existence, or where such control is restricted or curtailed to some degree[6]. Initially, when we consider the Individuals that would fit into this Circle, we may be considering those who cannot communicate their wishes - for example a person in a medically-induced coma - or those who have transgressed a society's laws, whether formally recognised or not, and who are consequently not allowed to participate freely in society. However, this also includes those situations where the Individual lacks the required resources to carry out what we would consider to be the normal activities of existence and therefore has no direct control over such an existence, being instead reliant on the support of others. In early forms of society, this may include an Individual that has none of their own tools for hunting or for making those items that they require to survive and must depend on others to

---

[6] It should be noted that in the UK, those under the age of 16 are not considered to be part of the Circle of Dependent Control as they would normally come under the Individual Unit that includes their parents/carers. In other society's, this age may be different.

provide them. It would also include those who are no longer capable of carrying out the tasks of basic survival due to illness or infirmity.

In the modern capitalist society, the Individual may also lack either the finances or the control over their finances to allow them to determine the basics of their existence. This may be as a result of a lack of employment, or finances being withheld (for example by a manipulative spouse, or through state controls over their benefits). They may be dependent on financial support from others such as friends or relatives or on the society in which they live developing some form of welfare support system. In Britain, in addition to the Welfare State, this would also include such historical practices as the use of Work Houses and the Poor Laws of the Victorian period. It would include anyone on state-derived, income-based benefits as well as those who, although fully-employed, are reliant on, for example, food banks in order to survive. Essentially, it includes anyone who is dependent on others or is dependent on the formal and informal welfare support systems of the society in which they live.

In addition to those who are completely dependent, this will also include those cases where people are partially dependent on others, either financially or legally. This would include, for example, those resident in care homes or half-way houses, those in refuges, those on parole or under the care of social services. Legal control may also be missing, meaning that a person is unable to determine what they can do, where they can go or what agreements they are able to enter into. Examples of this would be where the Individual has been deemed incapable of making decisions for themselves (such as where another Individual has been given power of attorney over them).

We may be inclined to regard the Dependent Circle of Control as a bad thing, a place where we are unable to function as we would expect or want. Such a way of thinking is possibly a reflection of how we understand such forms of dependency within our own societies. In some social systems, all Individuals would fall into this category because all of the requirements that a person may need in order to maintain their existence are collectively owned by the society and shared according to the needs of each. In such societies, the Circles of Dependent and Personal Control may merge together with those of Communal and Societal Control because each Individual has become inseparable from the society as a whole. Everyone is included within all areas of society and, while there may be nominal leaders, decisions are taken collectively and without anyone being excluded from that process. It should also be made clear that any modern society that wasn't providing support for those of its members that need it may be on shaky grounds identifying itself as a functioning society.

2.2.2 Personal Control

The second Circle of Control is the Personal. At the level of Personal Control, the Individual has control over those resources that give the sense that a person has the idea that they have freedom and control over their existence. They have a degree of choice over what to do with their time, the kind of work that they wish to undertake and the way in which they and their family live. In early forms of society, they would have the skills and resources to ensure their own survival, and while they may also participate in the collective sharing of resources, the fruits of their labour are generally directed towards supporting their own existence first and foremost. In the modern capitalist society, the Individual will be able to control their personal finances in so far as these stem from the value of the labour that they provide and they can determine to some extent what that income is spent on. They will have the right to enter into agreements, both formal and informal, with others as well as taking on the related responsibilities for upholding their part of the bargain: As well as being allowed to make decisions over their lives, they are also held directly accountable for the decisions that they make.

Within the Circle of Personal Control, the Individual is no longer dependent on others or upon wider society for their immediate survival needs and to some extent we can find the beginning of a distinction between the Individual and society, that is, the person is able to take on their own identity as a separate entity outside of society. Such a state of being is what we would consider 'normal' within our current understanding of our own lives and the societies in which we live, perhaps seeing it as the natural progression from a state where we are dependent on a wider social network[7]. However, what this also brings with it is a state where, just as we are able to begin to choose the extent to which we participate in society, so that wider society is also in a position to determine the limits it will place upon us as a result of those choices, and to begin to impose legal demands on the members of a society as part of the requirements set out as what are effectively the rules of societal membership.

---

[7] One issue that has been identified in relation to the increasing separation between the Individual and Society is the gradual breakdown of communal support available from friends and relatives, especially in relation to new families.

2.2.3 Communal Control

The third Circle of Control is the Communal[8]. Here, the Individual is now able to exercise control over other Individuals within the community in which they live. The power that is enabled within this Circle allows control over other Individuals beyond the limits of the holders own Individual Unit. This is achieved through either the ownership of resources that form an essential element in the existence of other Individuals at a Personal or Dependent Control level, or it is achieved through the granting of power over those resources, by whatever means, that allows for the same decision-making control to be exercised.

The Individual enters a position where they are able to exercise direct control over those outside of their immediate Individual Unit through the application of decision-making control over exploitable property that is required by others in the maintenance of their existence. Whereas within early societies, we find the possibility for a sharing of common resources or a 'fair exchange' of services from one to another, at the level of Communal Control within the modern capitalist society, we see Individuals being able to make the decisions on how other people are able to access these resources in

---

[8] The word 'Communal' is used in the sense that control extends beyond the Personal and into that of the wider society.

such a way that they are able to exploit the needs that another will have for them for their own profit.

In earlier forms of society, we would expect to see a collectivised approach to this type of control where items are shared with others in exchange for some form of benefit in kind. For example, in Amish communities, this appears in 'barn-raising' community activities where an Individual will provide their labour and skills to help in the construction of a building in exchange for a similar return of labour and skills from other members of the community in the constructing of a building that they require.

Once we get into what are often regarded as more 'advanced' forms of society, this type of community-based bartering makes way for a less equal system of exchange, where the exploitation of property involves the establishment of an arbitrary value above and beyond any labour involved in its attainment. For example, accommodation will be rented or mortgaged to an Individual not in relation to the cost to the owner of any labour involved in building or maintaining the property but for an arbitrary 'current market value' that allows the owner to accrue greater wealth. In relation to mortgages, if the Individual is able to maintain their payments throughout the duration of the agreement, they may eventually come to own the property. However, within the rental market, what we find is that there is an increasing application by landlords of the use of above-mortgage-value rental rates so that the Individual not only pays sufficient to pay the landlord to own the property but may also find themselves paying to cover additional amounts that effectively covers any extra costs that the landlord may accrue, ultimately seeking to include their own living expenses. Landlords will then continue charging those same amounts even after the value of the property has been met so that they can accrue further wealth. What we see, therefore, is an increasing system of parasitism within the rental market where landlords acquire properties and have renters pay not just for the labour involved in the landlord "being a landlord", but also so that the landlord can pay off any debt that they have taken in relation to the property, and then continuing to demand the same amounts so as to acquire greater wealth for themselves.

This Circle of Control will also encompass those people in workplace positions that allow them control over hiring, promoting or firing staff and judgements over pay increases. Effectively, the 'property' that is controlled is not something tangible and physical but is rather an abstract concept that is inherent to the position that the Individual holds.

Holding power within the Circle of Communal Control is not necessarily a malignant characteristic. It is possible to have control over such communally-based property without exploiting the needs that others may have in relation to it. However, with all societies that operate under a capitalist economic system, the exploitation of such property becomes a necessary feature in its ownership. Even where an Individual chooses not to exploit the excess property that they own, where a landlord, for example, keeps their properties empty to avoid exploiting any potential tenants, they are effectively reducing the available housing stock, thereby causing rents to artificially inflate.

2.2.4 Societal Control

The fourth level of control is Societal Control. This is where power extends over a much wider section of the population of a society, or over the entire population. Within this Circle of Control, the Individual is able to participate in the control of others beyond those other Individuals whose needs can be exploited through the ownership of property and to those Individuals that they may never have any direct contact with but whom they can control through the ability to make or enforce the rules by which the society functions.

Within early forms of society, this Circle of Control would include, perhaps, those considered as elders or tribal leaders who would understand the history of their society, be able to define and interpret the correct social practices, and clarify the nature of their belief systems so as to guide others on how they should live their lives. Such forms of power can be seen as integral to maintaining the fabric of those societies through a collectively shared understanding of their universe. Very often, the same systems are used to maintain the mechanisms of social control in modern societies, even where there is no longer a valid reason to be found for maintaining such mechanisms, for example through the exploitation of terms like "traditional values" in order to exploit the idea that the established order is both the best form of society and a natural state of being.

If we look at modern societies, we can see the forms of Societal Control in the development and structure of governments - both local and national - with their accompanying civil service, through the security and judiciary services (especially in the complex formalities of legal language and behaviours demanded), and through the maintenance of an economic system by which the state organises itself and applies its rules to the wider population. We still see the application of what can be considered as a unifying belief system in ideas such as 'democracy' or 'free markets' that are expected to be taken as universal truths. The expectation of acceptance is simply a tool to support systems of social control.

Such tools of social control will impact on the Individual in various ways: at a financial level, for example through taxation; at a legal level through the formulation of laws governing how the Individual is required to behave; and, within some societies, through controls imposed upon education, media, and political/religious belief in order to control what people think. Within early forms of society, the structures of social control would normally form part of a collective means by which cohesion can be maintained in order to ensure collective survival. However, once societies began to develop more complex forms, it becomes increasingly possible to create mechanisms by with specific groups of people or sections of society can be formally controlled. It ceases to be about the society's survival but about the survival of an established order within the society.

These tools of control are utilised to ensure that the rules only apply to certain groups rather than to everyone within a society. In such cases, what we often find is that there are means by which those who hold Societal Control are able to absolve themselves from the same processes of legal accountability that are applied to those who are controlled. Such would be the case in, for example, the Boris Johnson government in the UK or in the Stalin-led government in the Soviet Union while it operated under an economic form built upon principles of state capitalism. In both examples, the society's leaders were responsible for the deaths of large numbers of their own population but no legal action was ever taken against them.

2.2.5 Global Control

Finally, there is the Circle of Global Control. This is the Circle of Control within which a society is controlled by external forces that the average person would have little knowledge of and no access to influence. It is the means by which globally influential organisations wield power over all of a society's functioning mechanisms. An example of such control in early societies can be seen in the way that an invading external force may remove or destroy resources, take slaves and thereby reduce the size of a population to critical levels or demand that 'tribute' be paid to the conquering force, thereby reducing the resources available for the survival of the defeated society. Such methods of applying Global Control continue to be employed in modern societies. Examples of this can be seen in the attempts by Nazi Germany to destroy Warsaw and eradicate the Polish intelligentsia, or in the US carpet-bombing of Laos to prevent the area being used by the North Vietnamese to the extent that fifty years later, the bombing is still claiming victims. More recent examples would include the invasions of Iraq by various western governments and Gaza by Israel in order to secure gas and oil reserves.

We can also include with this Circle of Control those cases where nations will impose colonial control on another, imposing laws, restrictions or seizing resources through the imposition of trade regulations and limitations. We can see examples of this in the control imposed on the West Bank, the invasion and colonisation of Tibet by China, the colonialism by Britain of India and China, and in the economic blockade of Cuba by the USA.

However, there are also those methods of control that have been determined by various organisations as 'acceptable' processes. This would include, for example, the governance of oil prices by OPEC, restrictions placed on the ability of a nation to trade with other states by the World Bank and the impositions placed on a society's economic structures by the IMF.

2.3 Models of Control

While Fig. 2 presented a version of the Circles of Control where the system has each Circle placed concentrically within the next, this is only one possible format that control within any given society can take. In order to identify the control model for a society, it is necessary to look at what people would be contained within each of the Circles of Control, whether there is fluid movement between each of the Circles and how each relates to the others. Consequently, there can be various models for the distribution of control within society, with each variant indicating a different class structure.

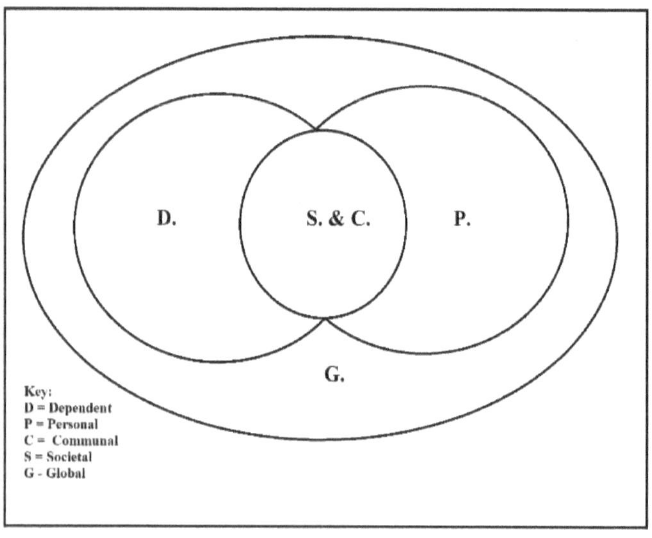

Fig. 3: Dual Leadership Society

In Fig. 3 we have the presentation of a 'dual leadership' society. While a society at the peak of its potential development may be one where all members of the society would have an equality of power over the mechanisms that affect the existence of the Individual, and where all people would exist within the Circle of

64

Societal Control, able to exercise control not only over their own existence but also over the properties that enable communal levels of control, this society has split into two factions – those who are dependent on society and those who hold Personal Control – with the two groups sharing the decision-making process at both the Societal and Communal levels. This would also mean that those who are dependent on society for the means to control their own existence would also have direct access to the Societal Circle, and that while they may require the support that allows them to function fully within society, they are also firmly embedded within the decision-making processes that impact both themselves and society as a whole. Global control still sits beyond their reach since this would normally be outside of any society's ability to exercise its own influence. However, in such a society, it would be expected that all Individuals would have an input into any and all negotiations with those external global organisations, should such a circumstance arise.

By looking at the Circles of Control as they apply within a society, it is possible to develop a complete understanding of the control structure that is in place and the position of each Individual within it. In the following sections, we can see how the Control Model can be applied to various historical societies.

2.3.1 Hunter-Gatherer Society

The following describes two applications of the Control Model (Fig. 4 and Fig. 5) as applied to two possible forms of hunter-gatherer society. As with all societies, even within what we would like to consider a 'primitive' form of society, we have the same Circles of Control: Dependent, Personal, Communal and Societal. And beyond the control of the society, as with all, there is the Circle of Global Control.

In Fig. 4, we see a tribal community where, in addition to everyone holding Communal Control over their collective resources, everyone also shares in Societal Control, with decisions affecting the whole community being discussed by all members and a shared

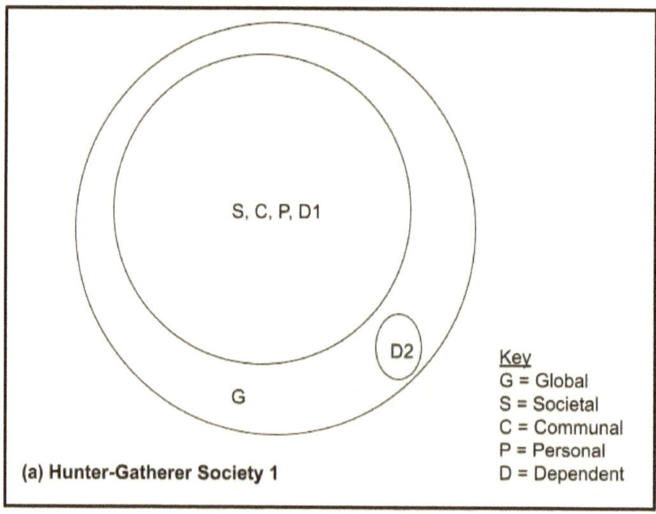

Fig. 4: Hunter-Gatherer Society 1

agreement being reached. The society also shares its knowledge and wisdom through community story-telling and methods of re-emphasising oral history in order to unify the whole group and maintain a sense of collective belonging. However, due to the often precarious nature of their existence, those who fall within the Circle of Dependent Control are split into two groups: D1 sits within the core of the society, within the community, while the other, D2, sits tangential to it. Those that are no longer able to provide for themselves and who have no close relatives within the society that will support them, while still taken care of when food is plentiful, will find that, when resources become scarce, they are cast out from the society and left to fend for themselves, that is, they are left to die[9].

In Fig. 5, we have a society where social cohesion is maintained through the knowledge held by tribal elders. As they hold the full knowledge of their history within their own group and pass the interpretation of that knowledge to the rest of the tribe as and when required, as guidance, through stories, and through a shared belief

---

[9] There are a number of myths and legends from across the world that make use of such events due to it being an intrinsic part of their collective histories, for example the Inuit legend of the birth of Nuliajuk, the goddess of the seas, who had once been an old woman who the community could no longer spare the resources for.

system, this group within the society sit within the Circle of Societal Control. Within the rest of the society, we have a shared, commonwealth of purpose, to the effect that all of their property is effectively shared by the collective, by those within the Circle of Personal Control, as well as some of those who would fall within the Dependent Circle who are able to still actively contribute to the organisation of such. As with all societies, there remain those who are entirely dependent on the society's collective support but they still form an integral part of that society.

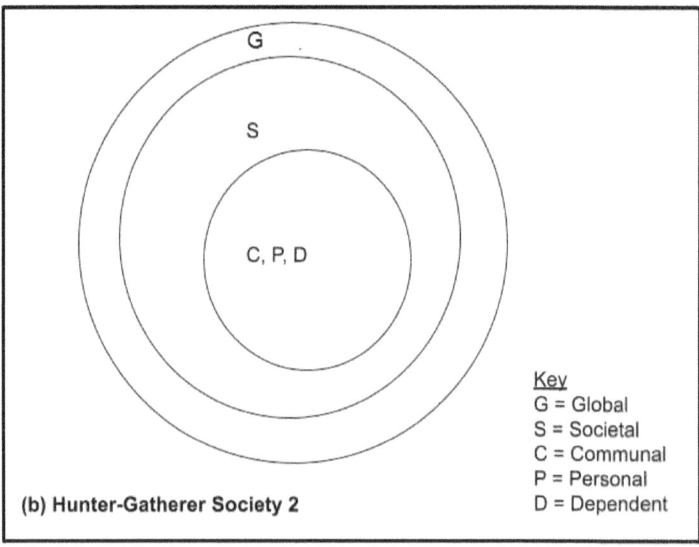

Fig. 5: Hunter-Gatherer Society 2

In both these examples of possible Hunter-Gatherer societies, the Circle of Global Control sits outside of the ability of the tribe's members to control. It may be that they have many good relations with the other tribes that inhabit the territories in which they exist. However, it is also possible that other, stronger tribes may seek to come into that territory and take whatever they can.

2.3.2 Roman-Britain

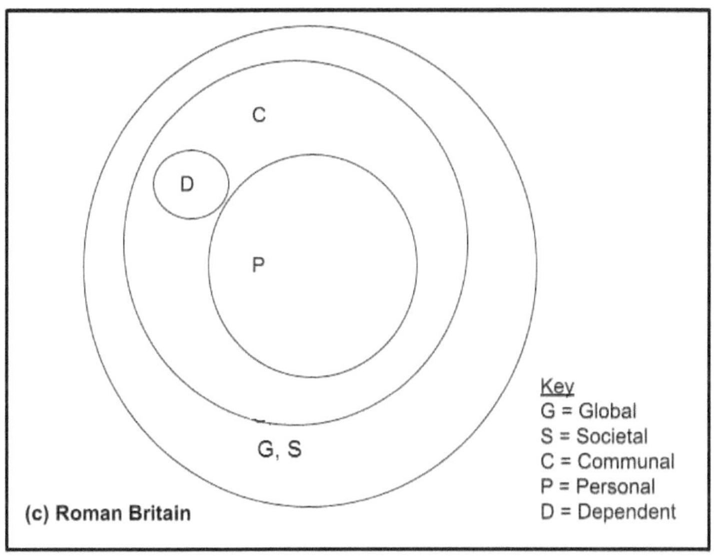

Fig 6: Roman Britain

In Fig 6 we have a depiction of society following the second Roman invasion. Immediately, we can see a clear distinction between this and the previous depictions within the Hunter-Gatherer societies. As a society that is now under external rule, the impact of the Circle of Global Control becomes clear. Roman rule - directed by Rome and enforced by the Roman military - has superseded all previous decision-making at the Societal level and people are now under a different set of constraints. While much may not change for the majority of ordinary people who were not exported as slaves, brutalized or murdered, in terms of the laws which are generally to be found in most societies - for example, those against randomly killing others - we have clear divisions between rules that apply to those who are the new rulers and those who are the ruled over, who would be included within the population of Ancient Britons.

Communal Control is now split between those Britons who have been allowed to continue to keep some or all of their lands (in return for cooperating with Roman rule) and those among the Roman invaders who have been given the lands of those who were not willing to cooperate. Those who were unwilling to cooperate may find themselves subject to various outcomes. Death or slavery would be the most likely, or if they were willing to adopt the acceptable behaviours, they could survive by becoming Romano-Britons. For the population of Ancient Britons, this would be the only way that they could sit with the Circle of Personal

Control. For these, the section of Communal Control in which they sit may greatly impact on the quality of their existence. Those who fall under the continuing rule of a local leader may find themselves in a better position than those living under the direct rule of a Roman, but they are still in essentially the same position of controlling some aspects of their lives but without the power to make any real decisions in regard to their society or to take any control over the land on which they live.

Once again, we have people dependent on society and who are reliant on their wider society for their survival. While those with relatives who are able to provide for them may be fortunate, many will fall under the care of the community within which they live, with many existing on the fringes of society, for example as beggars or thieves and subject to the applicable laws and punishments of whomsoever enforces them in the area where they are caught.

2.3.3 Feudal Europe

As Europe made the gradual transition to feudalism and monarchies began to be accepted as the rightful rulers, once again the Circle of Global Control moves beyond the society to those outside entities - usually other nations - that would be likely to invade. Societal Control sits with the monarchy and, to a lesser extent, those members of the monarch's close associates and those privileged appointees as regional rulers. Communal Control sits with these regional barons that the monarch has put in place to keep order and to ensure that the required resources are passed back to the crown. While there would be those whose specialist skills set them at a greater advantage, allowing them to form the first guilds, Personal Control is generally only held by those who would be willing to work under the terms of feudal serfdom.

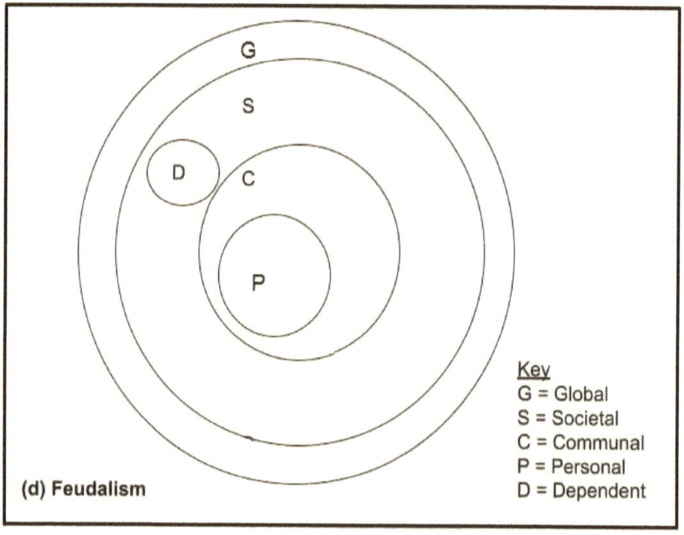

Fig. 7: Feudalism

Dependency once again forms a precarious position in society, but we also have a greater number of people beginning to survive on the fringes of society, as well as

72

the beginnings of charitable societies – most often closely tied to the organised religious groups in each area.

2.3.4 State Capitalism

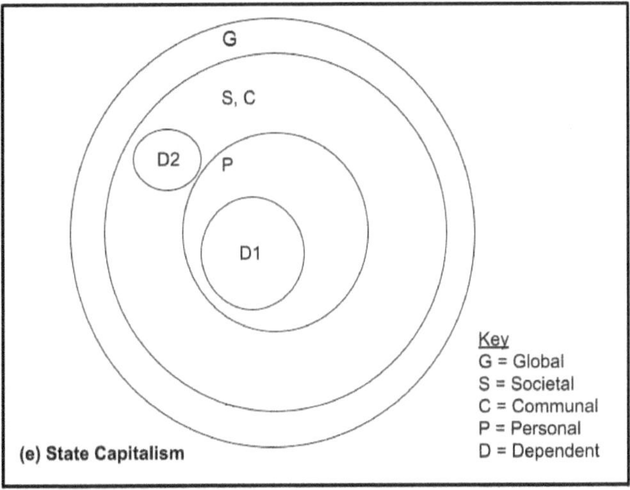

Fig. 8: State Capitalism

The Model of Control shown in Fig 8 demonstrates a society under the economic system of State Capitalism, such as that which existed under Stalin in the Soviet Union. While most often perceived as a form of communism, the economic model used during this period of the Soviet Union's history did not involve a shared ownership and distribution of resources but rather maintained ownership, control of distribution and the holding of all excess as profit by the state "on behalf" of the people. While this should have meant the organised form of equal ownership and distribution that the state claimed, what actually happened is that the Soviet state - that is, the system of civil servants, bureaucrats and polit-bureau officials - took ownership of the sum total of production, shared only what was absolutely necessary (and in the case of the Ukraine famines, not even this was done) and retained the rest to be enjoyed by themselves. While it can be argued that this method of unequal distribution enabled the Soviet state to defeat Nazi Germany in the east, it also contributed to a great many deaths as a result of state-inflicted shortages of resources. Again, we find that there are two distinct groups of those who should be considered as dependent: those who are cared for by the state or by their relatives, friends or neighbours; and those who have fallen foul of the state. For many in this latter group, death was always a highly probable outcome, but it could also mean the likelihood of becoming part of the gulag penal system.

2.4 From Modelling Control to Identifying Class

Having established the different areas by which the Individual can exercise control over their own life or that of others, we next need to consider how this would then translate into a class system. As previously mentioned, the existing models for describing class have failed as they are either too vague to be of any use or are so splintered into such minute detail that we cease to be dealing with class at all, and all too often they portray a misleading set of social relationships between the people in one class and those in another.

Leaving the Circle of Global Control to one side, as this will generally sit well beyond the reach of most members of society, including a large portion of those who hold Societal Control, we have 4 areas to consider. We can then apply to these the descriptors that identify the key functions fulfilled within society of those that sit within each Circle of Control. In order to do this, we need to work through a number of straight-forward questions in relation to the way that the society functions within this model:

a) Which people sit within each Circle of Control?
b) Are people being placed within their Circle by the circumstances of their existence or by socially imposed conditions?
c) What is the social relationship between those in one Circle of Control and those in another?
d) Is there free movement between one Circle of Control and another?

If we take the example of those who exist in the two Circles of Dependent Control in the first example of Hunter-Gather society (D1 and D2 in Fig. 4) as our example, we can begin to demonstrate how these questions can form our understanding of the class system within that society.

In answer to the first question, those within D1 are the close relations of those within the Circle of Personal Control, whereas those in D2 have no close relations within that Circle. Those in both D1 and D2 are recognised as valued members of the society due to the time that they have spent within it and the contributions that they have made over many years.

When we come to the second question, we find that while those in both D1 and D2 sit within the Dependent Circle due to their old age and failing health, the split has occurred due to socially imposed conditions: those in D2 have no close relatives remaining alive. While the society as a whole recognises the past contribution of those in D2 and values them for the knowledge that they have built up, the skills they once had and the stories that they can tell, when food is shared after a hunt, the choice cuts of meat will not be passed to them. Everyone, including those in D1, will receive a more sustaining portion. Their lives have been reduced to one of subsistence.

When we look at the relationship between one class and another through the third question, we see that again there is a clear difference in the way that those in D1 and D2 are treated by other members of the society. Those in D1 are part of sustainable family units, fulfilling the role of grandparents within those families and having close bonds with them. Those in D2, however, although part of the tribe, have no close ties and while the rest of the tribe will join together to support them, this arises due to the nature of kinship, friendship and community within the tribe, and nothing further. What we may see is that the first ones to help and assist those in D2 are those who – while still fit enough to hunt, build, make tools etc. – are single, having lost their own close family due to adverse conditions, illness or accident over the years. These Individuals will hold a particular sense of kinship for as long as circumstances allow because they know that the same fate may await them in years to come. Due to their collective histories and experience, everyone within the tribe – including those in D2 – knows that they are in a very vulnerable position.

When we answer the final question, we see that, we have a society where everyone participates in Societal, Communal and Personal Control, so free movement between the Circles does not appear to be an issue. While the whole tribe may gather to discuss what to do for the coming season, those in D1 and D2 both share their knowledge of the most favourable hunting grounds for the weather to come but everyone is fully aware that those in D2 speak as much from self-preservation as they do from experience. They may suggest a different path to anyone else, not because it leads to better resources but because they know that the other route is too difficult and they may not survive the journey. In the end, while their thoughts may be respected, they are unlikely to be heeded unless the whole tribe is in agreement with them.

What we have then in D1 and D2 are two distinct classes arising. Those in D1 form the basis of a Dependent Class. While they may have knowledge and experience that can benefit the whole tribe, this is very much based in the past with less relevance to those with more current experience. As citizens within the society, they are valued as close kin, but without the ability to help in many of the activities needed for survival, the best that they can hope for is to be seen as informal 'elders'.

Those in D2, however, are in a different position. While just as reliant on the rest of their community as those in the Dependent Class, they lack the close kin relationship of those in D1. If the tribe does not provide them with their own places to live, they will be put with anyone who may have space, or will sleep with the tribe's nominal leader who takes them in out of a sense of community duty. With no one to take care of them or to look out for their needs, they are at the mercy of the whole tribe and depend upon the goodwill of all for their survival. Effectively, in addition to being dependent, they have become outsiders within their own tribe. For this reason, they now form a Dependent Outsider Class, existing on the fringes of society.

THE CLASS SYSTEM IN BRITAIN

Introduction

So just what counts as a worker? Is class a matter of 'white collar' versus 'blue collar'? And who the hell are those that we keep calling the 'bourgeoisie'? As previously noted, class cannot be defined in terms of interconnected, hierarchical social structures, which would lead us back to that mythical 'ladder' but should be viewed instead in terms of the way that the Circles of Control are organised within a society and the systems of social control that are then used to link or divide them. It is possible that a class system could be hierarchical, or even classless, but it is not necessary. Only once we look at the form that the Circles of Control take, can we begin to consider the composition of those classes and why certain people only have control within specific Circles and whether they are actively prevented from having any access to the others. These Circles of Control give us the key to understanding class relationships and allow us to determine how the class system functions.

Whether it is the gradual rebuilding of systems after the Bronze Age Collapse, the restoration of whole nations after war or the rebuilding of cities after natural disasters, people have sought to regain some semblance of order, something that resembles to some degree that which they understood from before. The architecture may change, the political and economic structures may differ, but ultimately people seek to return to a state in which they have access to food and shelter, structure to their lives and a form of order that allows them to continue without fear of what the following day may bring. Within such attempts to create order in our lives, it is possible to see a wide variety of potential social structures and systems developing, but one look at the Western world - so full of the opportunity to reset their society through civil wars and revolutions - and it seems to be that each society has found its own path to a similar end point: From chieftains and kings, feudalism, early forms of restricted government - both alongside monarchy and without it - and finally towards a form of representative democracy. And within each society that has moved its way along such a path, we find that we have a gradual development of the capitalist economic system whereby the familiar economic and class divisions have also formed.

It needs to be recognised at this point that while the need for people to develop structures and order from what they experience as chaos is a natural process of human existence, the social and economic structures that are formed are not causally related to such a need. The rise of varying forms of capitalist economics within these societies appears to relate much more to the lack of social movement over many centuries and the fact that those with some element of Societal Control will try to exploit their position for their own benefit. The similarities between those societies that share these features would suggest that we might expect to find similar class structures. In our previous analysis of these various histories, sociologists have tried to define the different systems in terms of a class structure that sets them apart from our own. For the classical civilizations, they will be defined by emperors, caesars, kings, the ordinary citizens and slaves; the middle ages, we will talk of kings and barons and serfs; and prior to the Industrial Revolution we have the agrarian workers, the skilled craftsmen, and yet more kings. This definition of roles in ways that keep the past at arm's length works wonders as a way of disguising class systems and masking the structures of control that define them, allowing us to show that we have made an unending stream of progress in the way that our societies are organised. However, if we take a closer look at the collective histories of Europe, what we see is that there are always those living at the very bottom, the poorest of the poor who must depend on others for their survival; we have those whose only function seems to be to work, from the moment they are able to until the day that they die; and then we have those who have control over those beneath them - the barons, the landowners, the landlords with the kings, the queens and the governments sitting atop it all. The people occupying each layer may differ from one incarnation of society to the next but there are always these same levels.

What needs to be understood what is the defining link between these different descriptions of these four levels actually is and for this we need to go back to the way in which our societies reform after they have been pulled apart. What we have is a desire to return to order, as quickly as possible; we desire a form of order that we feel protects us from the threats that our very existence brings; and above all we desire something that allows us to live in safety. These become our priorities in times of trouble, and such needs can be exploited. This is because the other thing that is often found in such times is the desire that some will have to restore their ability to exercise control over others, to have power and the associated wealth that comes with it. What we find in almost all societies where fundamental change has taken place is that those involved in causing this change to occur can usually be found in the place of those that they have sought to be rid of. Whether it is Roman emperors being murdered by their successors, Washington finding his place as the first US president, Lenin and Trotsky taking control in the Soviet Union or Mao Tse Tung becoming the first leader of the People's Republic of China, it is a very rare thing to find those provoking social change handing over the reins to those they will have lead. What we have, then, are a series of societies where, whenever the social systems change form, we still have the very poorest remaining poor; those who did the bulk of the work, still working solely as a means to survive; those who own the means that the workers need in order to live and those at the very top who wield the ultimate control over everyone else.

When we come to identify the different classes, rather than using the language that merely describes levels in relation to each other (for example, lower, middle and upper), it is important to identify the role that those in each class undertake within society in relation to each other. As previously stated, while every society can be analysed using the Control Model, not every society will display the same class structure because while the Circles of Control can be applied to each, the way that those with access to each Circle of Control relate to each other and their wider society may differ greatly.

3.1 The Control Model Applied to British Society

When we analyse British society using the Circles of Control Model, we find the following:

(1) There is a clear section of the population that receive state-derived benefits through unemployment-related benefits, state pensions, disability benefits and housing

benefits (among a number of others, without which they would be unable to survive). There is also a Care System in place (both within a nationalised system of support and with privately-owned services). In addition, we have a judicial system where the state holds people in state and private-run centres both on remand and following sentencing. All of this indicates the existence of a Dependent Circle of Control.

(2) There are a large number of people who work for a living, their entire existence being derived from the fact that they receive a salary in some form from the work that they engage in. This section of people may own property (or own a mortgage-debt on such property) that they inhabit or may rent their living accommodation. They will be employed by either privately-owned businesses - in some cases these are internationally-owned - or by the few remaining state-owned organisations. This group of people would make up those that we find in the Personal Circle of Control. However, we also have a substantial number of people within this group who, in addition to working, are also in receipt of state-derived benefits or charitable support in order to maintain their existence.

(3) Those that we would identify as working for a living have access to living accommodation through either taking on a mortgage debt for a property or renting accommodation. There is a limited supply of state-owned rental property across the entire country, much of it having been sold off with the councils that previously owned them being prevented from building new properties. The private-rental sector also operates a variety of mechanisms which prevent some people from being able to access such property. While the appearance of signs in windows stating "No Irish, No Dogs, No Blacks" seems to have become a thing of the past, we do find a lot of use of "no unemployed" - despite the fact that this would normally involve guaranteed rental income through the housing benefit system - and many cases of discrimination being applied by property owners against certain 'types' of people. While arranging a mortgage debt will involve the debtors saving up a substantial deposit, the rental market also requires that renters hand over a deposit which can be anything equivalent to between 1 – 6 months of rent. What this indicates is that there is a distinction being made between being able to work and being able to own property in which to live.

(4) Much of the property used for accommodation purposes is privately owned. There is what is referred to as a

'housing market' which, like all such markets is supposed to keep prices at an affordable level, but the lack of available property, the shortage of social housing and the fact that much of that property that is available is privately owned, means that this housing market does not function in the best interests of those who require housing but is entirely in the interests of those that own the properties. This has created a system by which property can be readily exploited, with rents often being in excess of what a mortgage-debt for the same property would cost. This indicates that there is a group who fit into the Circle of Communal Control who own such property and that they are actively exploiting those who need the use of this.

(5) While there are a number of trades unions whose core task is to ensure that their members receive a decent recompense for their labour, several of these do not appear to work in the support of their members, preferring instead to operate on the basis of ensuring that they retain positive relations with business leaders and a number of those that do actively campaign on behalf of their members have been targeted by government action in an attempt to restrict such activities. While this is the most obvious example of the presence of a two-strand, "carrot and stick"

approach to ensuring control over society, similar examples can also be seen in other areas of British society. In addition, it is possible to identify a judicial system which, in addition to supporting the state's legal system, also utilises its powers to prevent many forms of protest, regardless of the validity that such may have, if they do not agree with the established views of those holding Societal Control. As a consequence, we can see that there is both the application of enforced control and a degree of cultural acceptance of the subservient role of those with Personal Control which combine to restrict their access to Societal Control.

(6) Within the group that are identified as holding Societal Control, we find that, in addition to retaining the control over the society, much of Britain's wealth is also held here. At this level we also find a system of restricted access to Societal Control through the use of a system of representative democracy (approximately equivalent to a ratio of 1:100,000) which favours political parties over independent representation and where representatives are not actually required to represent any given viewpoint and, so long as the declared source doesn't conflict with the rules that they set for themselves, can take payments from anywhere. What we can immediately see is that Societal Control

is held by a very small section of society who utilise a system which is designed to ensure that a large portion of society will never be represented. This gives us a clear indication that there is a very definite split between those who hold Personal or Dependent Control and those who hold Societal Control.

What this analysis gives us is a Control Model of British Society as described in Fig. 9. In addition to the Circle of Global

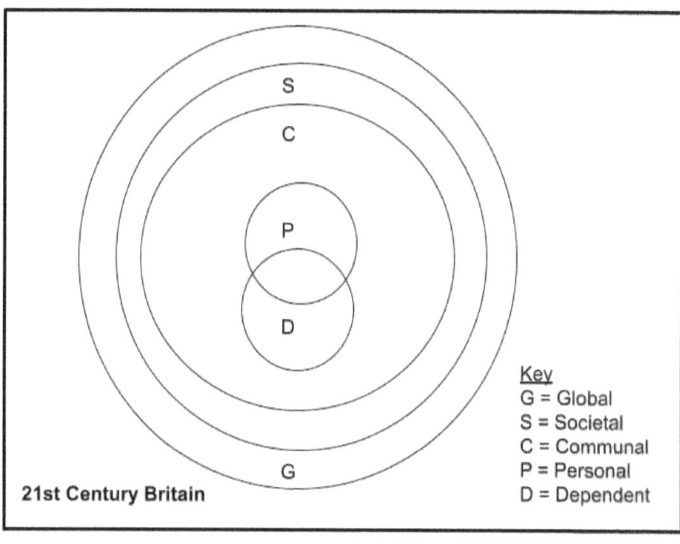

Fig 9: 21st Century Britain

Control, we have the four Circles of Control that we see in all societies, with the Personal and Dependent Circles of Control blurring together. Generally beyond the reach of these two groups is a Circle of Communal Control, where those included within this Circle will necessarily exploit those with Personal and Dependent Control and then, beyond this, we have the Circle of Societal Control which excludes access to the majority of society's members, regardless of whether they have Dependent, Personal or Communal Control. There is also some overlap between the Communal and the Societal due to the level of society's wealth that is held by those within the latter, much of it in the form of exploitable property. It should also be pointed out that some of those with Societal Control also have direct access to the Circle of Global Control, much of which is not shared with the rest of society beyond their own circle of associates.

In subsequent sections of this chapter, the class sections will be described in greater detail, but what we find when we measure British society against the Circles of Control is that we have the following:

(a) those with Dependent Control who, by virtue of their position, are largely unable to access all that society has to offer;

(b) those with Personal Control are only able to maintain a position within this Circle of Control by virtue of their labour and who are almost entirely unable to move up from this position to hold Communal Control due to the economic constraints of the system that they live under;

(c) those who have Communal Control by virtue of their ownership of exploitable property where the exploitation of the needs of others has become a necessary part of their position; and

(d) those who have Societal Control by virtue either of the position that they hold, wealth that they have accrued, or a combination of both and that this facilitates their continued domination of those who hold power in the other Circles of Control, with such domination being fully exploited to their own benefit.

Once we have established the basics of each of the Circles of Control within a society, we can then start to look at how each is composed and how they relate to those within the other Circles of Control. Rather than starting from the outer most Circle that is present, it is necessary to avoid starting with those who can wield Global or Societal control and to look instead at those who exist in the Circle of Dependent Control. The reason for this is that, in any society, those who hold control over others will always relate their version of this. What this is likely to do is create an analysis of a society in terms of the way that those who control it *want* it to see seen since this will enhance their ability to control that society. For example, if we look at the role of the *divine rule of kings* in the history of the British monarchy, if we are to accept this as the true reason for a monarch holding supreme control, then it ceases to be an element of the society's class system but begins to become an element of the natural order of things, no different from the impact of the weather.

So, beginning with those in the Circle of Dependent Control, what we notice is that rather than just including those who are no longer capable of caring for themselves (for example the elderly, the seriously ill, those in custodial care), we also have a number of others who are dependent because of the way that society functions. We have a large number of unemployed for whom the functions of the economic system's job market has rendered them as excess to society's needs; we have those whose control has been take away through various forms of abuse; and we have those forced into forms of 'social dependency' due to discrimination applied against them. Immediately, we are presented with a distinction between one section of society and the others.

There is also a clear overlap between the Personal and Dependent Circles of Control, resulting from the huge growth in what is commonly termed the *working poor*, that is, those who work to provide a living for themselves and the Unit to which they belong but, due to the nature of the economic system, cannot actually earn enough to make ends meet. While they may appear to have Personal Control over their existence, in many cases, this control is achieved only through additional external support through benefits, short-term, pay-day loans, familial assistance, food banks etc. We have then, a whole system of legally and financially bound forms of ownership that, as well as allowing for the exploitation of those who need access to such property, reinforce that exploitation through the mechanics of the economic system. Atop this, we have those who wield Societal Control where inclusion within this group is often legally and financially restricted, thereby minimising social mobility.

Having identified how these four Circles of Control relate to each other within British society, we can then begin to identify the class-relevant terminology that most accurately describes how each group functions within society. This analysis gives us the following terms:

    (i) those with Dependent Control who are reliant on others in some form to be able to achieve any level of Personal Control form an **Underclass**[10];

    (ii) those with Personal Control who control their own existence through the work that they

---

[10] For an explanation of why this group are identified as the Underclass and not the Dependent Class, see p.83.

perform but do not hold any control over others in society form a **Working Class**;

(iii) those with Communal Control who are able to establish control over others through the ownership and exploitation of property form an **Owning Class**[11]; and

(iv) those with Societal Control who are able to extend control over others through their access to the mechanisms of society form a **Controlling Class**.

3.2 The Class Model for Britain

We are so used to reading images in particular ways, applying meaning according to the placement of the image on the page, that it is difficult to create a diagram that does not belie the heritage of the hierarchical design of models of class and, regardless of how often it might be stated that the class ladder is a myth, once we lift vertical diagrams out from any accompanying text, people will begun to envisage that ladder! Then, there

---

[11] An alternative description of the Owning Class would be the Exploiting Class, due to the parasitic nature of much of the process by which wealth is accrued within this class. However, due to the fact that similar forms of class-parasitism exist within the Controlling Class, I have chosen to use the term Owning Class due to the fact that the exploitation that they practise is based upon the ownership of property.

are the concepts and questions that will always arise with the vertical diagram: If we group each Class section from top-to-bottom on the page, are we also making a 'top-to-bottom' qualitative statement? If we place them from left-to-right, are we suggesting the possibility of linear progression? If we place the Working Classes at the top of the page and the ruling classes at the bottom, are we just being obtuse and contrary for the sake of a political agenda that we haven't yet revealed? Ultimately, none of these - nor any other additional interpretation – should be added to the positioning of the diagrams on the page. Any class system is, in effect, its own model and no amount of graphic trickery will ever do full justice. So, unless connectivity is shown in the diagram, no connectivity should be implied.

In an attempt to avoid the hierarchical 'ladder' trap, I have chosen a linear format to describe the British class system. The shapes representing each class are all of a similar size as a means to avoid comparisons of, for example, potential wealth of those in each group that occurs with pyramid designs with class or the size of population that is contained within them. It is important to note that there is no connection between the Working Class and the Owning Class. Those members of the Working Class who aspire to own property that will

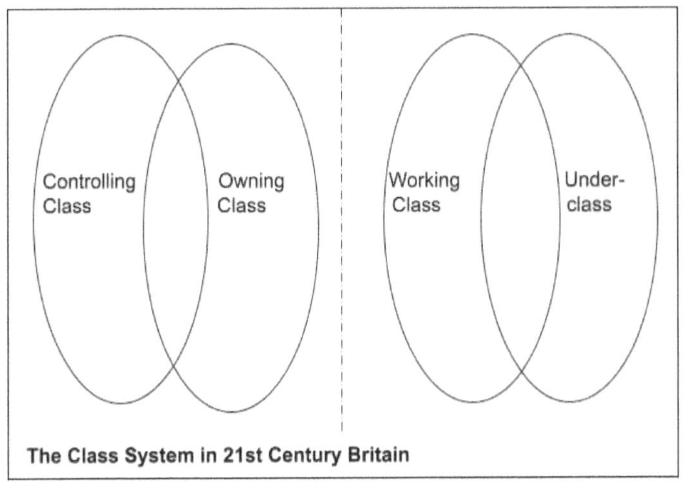

Fig. 10: The Class System in 21st Century Britain

enable them to exploit the needs of others but without sufficient wealth to do so remain members of the Working Class, regardless of what dreams they may have[12]. Similarly, those members of the Owning Class who find that the exploitable property they previously owned has gone, and they are no longer in a position to exploit the needs of others must be considered members of the Working or Dependent Class as appropriate.

---

[12] See section on "The Myth of the Aspirational Class" for a full explanation of how this works.

3.3 THE UNDERCLASS

So why is it that we need a different classification for this class of people? Why don't we simply refer to them as the Dependent Class, since they are identified as being dependent on society through the application of Circles of Control? In some societies, it would be very possible that such a class would take their name from the Circle of Control to which they belong, especially since their function within a society is reduced to one of dependency. However, when we move from the Control Model of society to the Class Model, it is necessary to look not just at the level of control that a group of people will have but to also look at the way that this class functions - or is allowed to function - within that society. As a consequence, when we look at the way that capitalist economies function, what we see is that those Individuals who only have Dependent Control over their existence function not just as those who are supported by society but also as those who can be used as a means by which society can be controlled. They are those who will be blamed first and forgiven last for any of society's ills, regardless of whether or not they have any direct impact upon such events. They are treated, first by those in positions that enable Societal Control and then by those within the rest of society, as a ready source of 'folk devil' through which people's attention can be guided away from those who hold the ultimate power over an Individual's existence. As a consequence, they can be said to sit "outside of" all other classes, hence the use if the term Underclass. While members of these groups may not perceive themselves as such, their position in society makes them vulnerable to abuse from both the state and other members of British society.

The term 'Underclass' comes from Swedish sociologist Gunnar Myrdel who first conceived the idea of a class that develops in any modern society outside of the formal class structures. I have used it as a consequence of the way in which those who fall within the Circle of Dependency are treated in Britain. Rather than consisting of those who are, for a variety of reasons, dependent on wider society for their well-being, as a result of infirmity, illness or legal status, this status is tied to their productivity, with them being identified not as being part of society but instead being regarded as a burden upon it. Their dependence is often deemed to be entirely of their own making and as a consequence they can be targeted by those in control as a parasitical entity, it being their fault that they are disabled, unemployed, poorly paid, growing old or just 'here'. This enables the Controlling Class to create a split between those who have limited or no control over their existence from those who are able to provide a level of Personal Control. The Underclass are, therefore, those who are not just dependent but also those whose dependence can be portrayed negatively within wider society.

As stated previously, while all societies can be analysed using the control model, not every society will have the same classes and class descriptors as another. For example, where a society capable of providing equitable support for all of those who would fall within the Dependent Circle of Control, actively treats those who are dependent as being at fault, and which uses the tools of discrimination to create deliberate divisions within society, it is doing so in order to transform a Dependent Class into an Underclass. We would, therefore, be unable to refer to the class containing those who are dependent as being the "Dependent Class" since, while such a class would consist primarily of those who are dependent on others to have any form of control over their existence - because of age, infirmity, disability or ability to work - the framework in which this dependency is treated by wider society means that they are no longer *just* dependent but are being actively and purposefully excluded, and as such different terminology must be applied.

What we have in Britain is a society that consistently seeks to discriminate against those who would be classed as dependent. Examples of this would be: the use of negative forms of language; the introduction of terminology such as 'benefits' to promote the idea of a person being a financial burden; the use of arbitrary sanctions to restrict their activities; the definition of some people as being 'less than' others in order to socially exclude them or to make them appear as less worthy members of a society. As a consequence, we can no longer identify them as a "Dependent Class" but must identify them by the way that the wider society is treating them: An Underclass.

3.3.1 Summary of Class Composition

Of the four class categories, this is by far the most complex as inclusion within it is not defined by a single over-riding factor, such as owning exploitable property or working for a living. Included within this class would be elements of financial and legal dependence, various forms of manipulation and victimisation, and the numerous cultural uses of demonisation to prevent some groups of people from having equal access to the benefits of British society. So the Underclass consists not only of those whose failing health places them in the weakest possible position in respect of their ability to control their own existence, but will also include those placed at a financial disadvantage, those who are unemployed, those denied access to all that society has to offer as a result of current trends in both official and cultural discrimination. As their status can be initially identified by having only Dependent Control over their existence, those Individuals who would fall into the Underclass will fall into one of the following categories:

    i.   the health dependent;
    ii.   the financially dependent;
   iii.   the legally dependent;
   iv.   the exclusionary dependent; and
    v.   the manipulated dependent.

i. Health Dependence

There can be many reasons for a person to be dependent due to their health. Long-term illness and old age would be the most common. However, any medical condition, whether physical or mental, can lead to a person becoming dependent on either other Individuals, on wider society, or both. This may just be a result of the onset of those infirmities that we associate with growing older, where a kindly neighbour may assist with getting to the local shops or where relatives make regular calls to check on someone's well-being. At this stage, we probably wouldn't include them as being within the Dependent Class, as such is the kind of support that we would expect from a community-minded society. However, one of the perils of a mortal existence is that our bodies have a habit of failing us more and more the older we get, often many years before we finally leave this mortal coil. Anyone with an understanding of common problems associated with old age: dementia, Alzheimer's, incontinence, and a whole range of other conditions will know that what may begin as a something requiring a little help here and there, can soon become a role for a 24/7 carer. Due to the way that the British welfare system has been designed - its intricate complexity and the many barriers that are placed in the way to prevent or stall claims - there are a large number of people in society who receive no official support and as a consequence are rarely considered to be dependents of any kind, despite this being the reality of their existence.

We also need to consider that there are many people with significant disabilities who would be classed as dependent due to their health. While many of them will be in full-time employment and will lead normal lives, the fact that they will face huge amounts of discrimination within society – both as a failure of ordinary people to act with any sense of decency towards others, and as a legislative and business failure to actually address inequalities – means that they are forced into a state of dependency on the acceptance and 'good will' of others. For example, many people with disabilities are paid significantly less than colleagues performing the same role who are considered able-bodied[13].

In addition to this, we still have a piecemeal approach to enabling those with disabilities to fully participate within society, with, for example, poor or limited provision for

---

[13] This is generally the reason why many companies tell their staff that they are not allowed to discuss their salaries with colleagues.

access to public buildings leading to wheelchair users being denied access.

ii. Financial Dependency

In modern Britain, any Individual who is financially dependent on others or on society – in part or in full – to achieve Personal Control, or anyone unable to achieve Personal Control for financial reasons, sits within the Underclass. This would include those who are entirely reliant on a society's welfare system for their means to exist. For example, an Individual in receipt of benefits in relation to their lack of employment, state pensions, or sickness, or for their housing costs to be met by similar benefits or support would be classed as financially dependent. In addition, we would include those who are generally excluded from the benefits system due to the application of formal sanctions or as a result of difficulty claiming benefits as often happens with, for example, homelessness.

However, between the Underclass and the Working Class, there is an area where financial dependence becomes an issue and the two classes overlap. While we may generally consider the Underclass to lack employment, this overlap will include many whose employment position does not provide an income that allows them to exist without being reliant on society. This would include:

- those working the equivalent of full-time hours (and often more) but where the wages they earn do not meet the minimal living standards or even subsistence;
- those working and in receipt of benefits and/or reliant on support from relatives to make ends meet;
- those in employment who regularly rely on food-banks to subsist;
- those in precarious or temporary employment where there is little or no job security and where they will regularly shift between employment and unemployment.

This final category will also include those working illegally, or working within illegal professions, for example those working within the prostitution industry, or those reduced to begging to survive. While these people may be earning enough to live on – or enough as determined by the government – the precarious nature of their income, and the fact that their survival is reliant on too many external factors, places them within the Underclass.

iii. Legal Dependence

Those who are legally dependent will have had another party take legal control of their activities. While an Individual may dispute whether such control is valid, such control will have been determined as valid given the laws by which society is managed. This group would include:

- those who are being held within the prison system, including those who are on bail and have had restrictions placed on their activities; those who have left the system but are still on probation; and those on registers following completion of sentence who continue to have restrictions placed upon them;
- those living within the care system who receive support from care services to manage their lives and finances;
- those who have had another Individual or organisation be awarded 'power of attorney' over them.

Legal dependency applies to any Individual that has had their legal rights to make their own decisions in relation to their existence suspended, removed, or transferred to another. It would also include anyone who has been sectioned and is being held in psychiatric care. Anyone seeking asylum as a refugee and awaiting the processing of their asylum claim - and as such is not allowed to work under British law - would also be included within this group.

The second group would include anyone for whom another person holds 'power of attorney' as well as the majority of adults who live under the social care system. In Britain, it would also include anyone between the ages of 16 and 18 who will fall under elements of adult law for certain regulations but who are also prevented from entering into many legal arrangements due to their age.

iv. Exclusionary Dependence

Stigmatised groups will always reflect the current trends in social prejudice within any society. During the late Victorian period, the influx of European Jews into the East End of London resulted in numerous attacks against them in the press, which had a direct influence on the rise in cases of physical attacks in the streets. At other times, it has been the place of Muslims, single mothers, the Irish, the GRT communities and new age travellers, Bangladeshis....[14] The list goes on. Society is seldom if ever without its stigmatised groups because they work so well as a means to create and maintain social division, disharmony and, as a consequence, control.

While those in stigmatised groups may have a good degree of control over their existence which would normally place them within the Circle of Personal

---

[14] It is important to stress that these groups are not included because of the nature of that group but because of the way they are treated by society as members of that group.

Control, their place within the Circle of Dependent Control arises as a result of the discriminatory treatment they face from the wider society. For example, while the majority of members of the GRT communities are working people and, in many cases, have a much greater degree of Personal Control over their existence than most of the rest of the Working Class, the use of both local and national laws specifically to target their choice of lifestyle, the closure of sites by local government, harassment by the police and also by those from local communities, all combine to create a system within which their freedoms and their available choices of involvement in society are restricted. It is this form of discrimination - both illegal and within the bounds of the law - that places those within groups within the Circle of Dependent Control and as such within the Underclass.

v. Manipulated Dependency

For a number of people, while they may be part of an Individual Unit and would normally sit within the relevant class that such a Unit belongs to, the way that they are treated by other members of the Unit places them as external to that class. This displacement results from what we would refer to as *manipulated control*, that is, another member or members of the Individual Unit uses forms of physical, psychological, sexual and financial abuse to control their lives.

The most common form of such manipulated dependence arises as a result of the controlling behaviour that forms a key factor of domestic abuse. While we may commonly associate domestic abuse with the easily identifiable physical threats or violence, these are rarely used just to inflict suffering but form part of a much wider process of ensuring control. As a consequence, the visible violence that may be seen is often just the tip of the iceberg, with much more going on at a covert, often subliminal level. Experiencing such manipulation can involve many things, including (but not restricted to): being restricted as to who they are allowed to see; having restrictions placed as to who they can have as friends or who within their family they may have contact with; having restricted access to their own or any collective income; or being controlled as to where they can go. As a result of this, the controlled Individual should always be considered as having access only to the Circle of Dependent Control, making them a member of the Underclass[15].

3.3.2 The Political Purpose of the Underclass

It is often considered one of the harsh realities of modern life that a 'few' people fall to the bottom of the

---

[15] It should be noted that the manipulator(s) does not, by virtue of their actions, automatically become a member of the Controlling Class.

illusionary social ladder. Commentators across the political spectrum will then wring their hands as they propose their latest idea to combat such eventualities, usually involving money being paid into the bank accounts of their friends and donors. The Underclass, however, are not an accidental feature of a modern society, but are an integral part of capitalist economies. The majority of those that 'fall' into such forms of dependency are not there by some freak of cosmic fate but are *placed* there in order to perform certain roles that are critical to the functioning of such an economic system. They perform two crucial functions: firstly, their financial poverty provides those in the Working Class with the incentive to keep working; and secondly, they can be used to facilitate divisions within the Working Class, thereby making control over the whole of society much easier to establish.

The greater the level of poverty among the Underclass, and the more precarious the financial status of the Working Class, the greater the fear that, should they fail to meet their targets, work above and beyond, or make work the purpose of their whole existence, they may also end up in that level of poverty. A badly paid job is thereby made much more preferable to no job at all. *"There but for the grace of god go I,"* becomes a common sentiment amongst the Working Class. As workers, unemployment ceases to be a period of stasis between gainful and fulfilling jobs but rather something to be truly afraid of, and a fearful workforce is a docile workforce: we do not complain, we do not ask for a raise and we do not go on strike for fear of what awaits us should we dare to ask for more.

While the main purpose of the Underclass is to create situational fear among the Working Class, their other key function is to be the target for any social-based anger within a society. In any society where there is a huge financial division between the Working Class and those holding Societal Control, the sheer weight of numbers of those with very little poses a distinct threat to those in control. A divisive society where wealth is held in the hands of the few will generate immediate friction and an angry population is a dangerous population. In such societies, the Underclass fulfils the role of becoming the target for much of this friction, thereby helping to deflect social unrest away from those who hold the most wealth.

As a consequence, those within the Controlling Class use their access to the media, to social commentators, to politicians, as the key weapon to target specific groups within both the Working Class and the Underclass. This is done in such a way that the rest will regard those targeted groups as the cause of their own problems. Newspapers will carry stories about, for example, single mothers or refugees being prioritised for social housing or those on disability or sickness benefits, or those receiving seemingly disproportionate levels of benefits 'taking' money from those in employment. We will be guided to view anything they receive as unfair on us and will be drawn into the already pre-established conclusion that such people are scrounging from society and depriving us of money. In such cases, very few examples will be given of genuine misappropriation but we will be guided to believe that this is the case for all such people. Headlines will tell the Working Class that what appears to be a massive sum of money is being paid to, for example, those with mental disabilities and our attention will be drawn to a couple of cases where an incorrect payment may have been made, presented in such a way so that we are lead to believe that every payment relates to a falsified claim. The Working Class are sold the idea that someone is getting "something for nothing" and since members of the Working Class are far more likely to come into contact with members of the Underclass than with those in the Owning- and Controlling- Classes, it becomes easy for them to spot such 'abuses' of the welfare system in their daily lives. What we don't notice that often, is those members of the Controlling Class who make fortunes and pay nothing back into society due to the many loopholes within the taxation system that they allow themselves to exploit.

In order to ensure that there is always a continuous supply of scapegoats, certain other groups will also be targeted, and as more vitriol is heaped upon them by the media, so the members of these groups who are not part of the Owning Class or the Controlling Class will become *de facto* members of the Underclass. Quite often, these groups will be selected on ethnic grounds as this makes them easy to identify. However, cultural and religious grounds may also be selected, especially where there is something easy to recognise, such as women wearing the hijab or mean wearing a turban. During the 1970s and 1980s, Irish people were targeted, along with Black and Asian communities. As the 1990s progressed, asylum seekers became the targets and as Britain entered the 2000s immigrants from Eastern Europe and those of the Islamic faith were singled out. As such distinctions are made, any benefits that these people may provide for the society are ignored in favour of sweeping statements and loose generalisations designed to whip up anger within the Working Class and to keep them fighting amongst themselves.

3.3.3 Summary of Features of the Underclass
1) the Individual is identified as holding Dependent Control over their own existence as a result of:
    i. Health Dependence;
    ii. Financial Dependence;

iii. Legal Dependence;

iv. Exclusionary Dependence; or

v. Manipulated Dependence

2) Dependency may be full or partial, but where it is partial the dependency will be long-term;

3) the society in which they live engages in various forms - legal or otherwise - of stigmatisation and discrimination for the purposes of social control.

3.4 THE WORKING CLASS

So what does it mean to be Working Class? Put simply, the Working Class functions in that capacity. In short, they *work*: They drive, they build, they teach, they nurse, they dig, they type, they clean… A list of Working Class roles in a modern society could go on endlessly. Gone are the days when we identified the Working Class solely by the calluses on their hands. There may be roles that appear to be easier, less stressful, better paid than others but what we need to recognise is that British society is divided into those who control the existence of others, those who own the means by which existence can be controlled and those whose only means to achieve any control over their own existence is through the value that is placed on their labour[16].

What distinguishes the Working Class from the Owning and Controlling Classes is that they are not in a position to extend their limited control over the lives of others.

The majority of people living in any modern capitalist society will fall into the Working Class. Within our analysis of British society using the Control Model, a group of people were identified who held Personal Control over their existence, but no further control over that of others.

---

[16] The omission of the Underclass from this statement is entirely intentional, in order to emphasise the fact that many of those within the Underclass who are working are deliberately excluded within society for specific political purposes.

This group of people form the basis of the Working Class. It would also include those family units where one or more adults are working as well as those households where a group of adults share a residence where each of the adults is working. The key defining features of those who would be classified as Working Class are that:

> (1) they only have access to the Circle of Personal Control and that this is achieved without recourse to support from either the state, charitable organisations, or their friends and/or relatives; and

> (2) their access to the Circle of Personal Control is achieved through their labour, either on-going or, in the case of those in receipt of state or work-based pensions, through their previous working history and that the nature of their work does not allow them to exercise control over others beyond the level of the organisation of their work.

There are several caveats that need to be clarified at this stage in relation to these two criteria. Firstly, in relation to (1), while they may work for a living, where this allows for the Individual to accrue extensive wealth through the acquisition of property that others require for their own access to Personal Control, they cannot be considered to be members of the Working Class. Likewise if the nature of their work allows them to have direct access to those in the Controlling Class, or where such work involves the active support of the Controlling Class, they cannot be considered to be members of the Working Class. In relation to (2), it should be noted that being in receipt of either a state or work-based pension only places a person within the Working Class if they did not earn this pension as members of either the Owning- or Controlling Classes and if the pension that they receive allows them to maintain a standard of living that would be comparable to that which they held while working and that they are not in receipt of additional support in order to achieve this standard of life[17]. As such, a member of the Working Class *must* work (or must *have* worked in the case of retired pensioners) in order to maintain an income that enables them to maintain the basic levels of control of their existence without recourse to other forms of support. To be Working Class effectively means having to *work for a living*. The Working Class do not work to extend control over others but solely to maintain a standard of living for themselves.

The position in society that is held by a member of the Working Class is determined by the fact that all control they hold within society is derived from the work that they perform and the earnings that they receive and that such control is limited to their own day-to-day existence. They are obliged to work to earn enough to live and while they

---

[17] However, what we find in most cases is that the state pension provides insufficient funds to provide anything but bare minimum subsistence and, as a consequence, most people receiving state pensions will find themselves becoming part of the Underclass.

may be in a position to choose the manner of their employment, they cannot choose not to be employed. Their control does not extend to those outside of the Individual Unit.

Ownership of property does not preclude someone from being included within the Working Class. Where such ownership is integral to their requirements to hold some form of Personal Control - for example 'owning' a home or a vehicle - and where the financial obligations involved in such ownership is met through the their own earnings, this would be included within part of the nature of their existence within an economic system based on capitalism. Such forms of ownership must also be solely a means to support their own existence and consequently would not form an exploitable resource.

So, the Working Class is comprised of those Individuals who are able to exercise Personal Control over their existence but have no control at the Communal or Societal levels. With such a system as capitalism, the Working Class do not work because it gives them meaning or purpose – a secondary benefit if it occurs – but because this is the only means open to them to have any form of control over their existence, and it is this control that gives the meaning and purpose. Work does not always necessarily provide an income on which a person can live a meaningful or purposeful existence, as control over such can still remain with others. While we would not consider such an existence as a form of slavery in the sense that we understand from an analysis of history, what we can see is a form of financially-controlled servitude, one that prevents the Individual from having full control over their existence and which mirrors earlier forms of the class system that we are told modern society has moved on from. Essentially, while we may not wish to admit it, to be a member of the Working Class is to fit into the same state of existence as the peasant farmers, sharecroppers and serfs of previous centuries.

Between the Underclass and the Working Class, there is an area where the two overlap. While we may generally consider the Underclass to lack employment, this overlap will include many whose employment position is tenuous:

- Those working full-time on minimum wage;
- Those working where their income is insufficient to cover their expenditure;
- Those in precarious or temporary employment where there is little or no job security.

3.4.1 Summary of Class Composition

A simple summary of those who would fall into the Circle of Personal Control, and consequently within the Working Class, will include the following:

(i) the ability to maintain a degree of financial independence as a result of the work that they undertake

(ii) holding no control over others outside the limits of their Individual Unit

As such, while a member of the Working Class is able to earn enough to be financially independent, they do not acquire wealth to the extent that they can control others.

i. Financial Independence

To be included within the Working Class, and not within any other class, an Individual must be financially independent in the sense that they can feed and accommodate themselves without recourse to any other support from elsewhere. In addition, this financial independence – and any wealth that they are able to gather – must not come through the exploitation of another Individual's needs or skills. Finally, any income that they receive must not be earned within a role that allows them to exercise either Communal or Societal Control. No Individual within the Working Class can ever be fully independent as their existence will always be controlled by the laws and policies of the society in which they live. However, they would be independent enough to make the basic decisions over their existence without reliance on any form of support from outside.

ii. Exclusion from Extended Control

Extended control means being able to control other Individuals. To be a member of the Working Class in modern Britain, an Individual must be able to be independent of additional support from others within society - or from society itself - but must also be in a position where they are unable to control the existence of any other Individuals. As such, any Individual who could be categorised as being a member of either the Owning Class or the Controlling Class cannot be a member of the Working Class, and as such must be excluded from having any extended control over other members of society.

3.4.2 The Political Purpose of the Working Class

All societies are completely reliant on the existence of a Working Class in some form. Whether those people are doing the hunting and gathering, ploughing the fields, mining the coal or typing at a computer, such work facilitates the functioning of the society and without it the society ceases to function and will collapse. The purpose of the Working Class is, therefore, to complete the work that society needs in order to function.

3.4.3 Summary of Features of the Working Class

The Working Class can be defined using the following criteria:

1) Their control over existence extends only over themselves and to some extent those who would be included within their Individual Unit. They have limited control over the entirety of their existence due to others holding Communal and Societal Control and can exercise no control over the lives of anyone beyond their immediate Unit.

2) Their control over their existence is derived entirely from the fruits of their labour.

3) Any property they own relates to their immediate working and living requirements and they do not own property which enables them to exploit the needs of others beyond their Individual Unit. They do not own exploitable property that could be used as a means to control or exploit the needs of others at a Communal level;

4) They do not hold Societal Control and do not have any influential access to those who do hold Societal Control.

3.5 THE OWNING CLASS

The Owning Class exists within capitalist systems like modern Britain in a different way to that which existed within earlier forms of society. In times past, ownership of any kind has been used to mark the defining quality of the ruling- and middle- classes with the development of social manipulation, ownership of aspects of property has become a key means in ensuring the continuance of class divisions. Rather than property being a social resource that is shared within the community, it was transformed into a privately-owned resource almost entirely under the control of the dominant class within the feudal system. It then becomes a private resource whereby other Individuals are permitted to have access to it in order to exploit the needs of others for their own profit. Anyone with the wherewithal can acquire such property, so that whereas the former allowed for very little societal change, the latter gives the impression of such by suggesting that anyone is able to gain access to the level of Communal Control. However, as we have seen in previous sections, ownership of a resource only allows for further exploitation if such is not required to support the Individual Unit in meeting their own needs. What we see within a modern society is that there is a clear distinction between types of property and between different forms of ownership, with some allowing the Individual to exist within society and others allowing for the exploitation of the needs of other Individuals within society.

The overriding factor defining an Individual's position within the Circle of Communal Control and within the Owning Class in Britain is that they own properties that others require access to, and that this is beyond that which is needed to maintain their own existence. Within the capitalist system, what this means is that they own property where the primary purpose of ownership is to exploit the needs of others, that is, the ownership of property facilitates the exploitation of other Individuals' needs in order to create wealth for the owner. A key identifier in defining this class is the disparity between the levels of wealth generated through ownership and the amount of actual labour performed.

This class will include many who may be perceived – either publicly or by themselves – as 'working for a living' but whose level of income does not equate to the amount of actual work that they put in, irrespective of their additional 'skills' that they bring to the role[18]. At the highest-earning levels, excessive salaries offered for such positions, more often than not, go to people already receiving similar salaries

---

[18] Usually, the justification for excessive salaries within certain sectors of business and politics is the need to attract higher calibre candidates for these positions. What we tend to see is that the same people rotate between different positions with directors of banks sitting in government, key officials being handed executive positions and an endless merry-go-round of people moving from business, to government, to civil service and back into business.

126

for similar positions elsewhere, ensuring that those with the greatest wealth can retain their wealth and position of influence, and also that access to this sphere of wealth and influence is restricted within the existing membership of the Owning and Controlling Classes. In times past, ownership of any kind has been used to mark the defining quality of the ruling- and middle- classes. With the development of social manipulation, ownership of aspects of property has become a key means in ensuring the continuance of class divisions.

3.5.1 The Issue of Ownership

Through the development of class theory, the question of ownership has been a means both to divide and to conquer. Whether identifying ownership of property as a means to stratify the classes, as the opposition to shared equality or as the sign that someone has managed to escape from poverty, the ownership of property has been a way of defining the *haves* and the *have-nots*. However, the simple definitions that have been used in the past to clarify property and ownership have long since lost their validity. When the Marxist concept of the 'means of production' was first voiced, the world separated easily into those who owned the land, the factories, the housing, and those who worked and lived in them. As the industrial framework of Britain has faded, business ownership has diversified so that we have multinational corporations owned by chains of parent companies at one end of the spectrum, where ownership is vague and encrypted, down to *micro-businesses* involving one or two people at the other where the only thing of any real value that is 'owned' is the idea of a business and the reputation it may have generated.

Clearly, there is a marked difference between the two, even though they may both involve the ownership of property. Where such ownership is vague and encrypted, however, the two have become blurred so that what Marx recognised as the bourgeoisie – the 'new money' owners of the industrial revolution who took control of the factories - has become synonymous with the family-run corner shop[19]. The impact of this has been to help obscure the higher levels of control in society by drawing attention to the visible, lower levels of possible control that the Working Class could identify as the main culprit for their exploitation. So instead of seeing business rates being raised by local councils or the economic failures of government, the eyes are turned to the shopkeeper, the one that the Working Class are most likely to encounter.

To add more potential confusion, we also have the growth in ownership of *abstract* property to contend with, such as intellectual property where it is possible to take ownership of an idea or the creation of an idea. But yet again, we have a distinction to be made in the ownership of

---

[19] Shops of this kind are rarely owned as a physical entity. The building will usually be rented and only the 'idea' of the business, the stock and the fixtures and fittings being owned.

abstract property held by the Individual as creator and the property held in the ownership of that same property for the purpose of exploitation. Once we acknowledge the need to include abstract property, we must also acknowledge that certain roles within society have specific, *abstract* powers attributed to them. For example, the monarch holds power by virtue of their position and must, therefore, be included.

What this simple idea of ownership needs to distinguish is the difference between forms of property that the Individual Unit requires to exist and those which can be used to exploit the needs of the Individual. However, property, of whatever kind, is often treated as an exploitable resource, regardless of whether it is required for the purpose of existence. As a consequence, if a building could be rented out to exploit the needs of another, regardless of whether the Individual requires it in order to have somewhere to live, it is treated as an indicator that they have entered the realm of the bourgeoisie. This would also include those people renting somewhere to live since they could also use their access to the keys to that property to rent it out to someone else for even more. Clearly, such a concept of property is deeply flawed.

Access to or ownership of property falls, therefore, into two main categories: that which is required by the Individual Unit for the purpose of going about their daily lives and that which is excess to this requirement and therefore becomes exploitable property. Exploitable property is not necessarily always being utilised as such but may be used to restrict access to property or simply to accrue value over time. There are several organisations which operate as financial institutions or provide retail services which operate on a system of collective ownership of their employees or account holders so that these Individuals are able to participate in the 'ownership' of the organisation. It should be pointed out that, due to the size of these organisations, the share of ownership held by the average employee, for example, is so insignificant that they effectively have no voice in the way in which the organisation operates.

3.5.2 The Exploitation of Property

What we have within the Owning Class is the exploitation of different forms of property to which they have such access as allows them the decision making power to identify who can and cannot use such property and at what cost. What we have are a set of forms of property that can be owned for the purpose of exploitation:

      (1) Ownership of accommodation;

      (2) Ownership of employment;

      (3) Ownership of ideas;

      (4) Ownership of utilities; and

      (5) Ownership of roles.

It is necessary to make distinctions between these categories in order to clarify the ways in which each can be used, whether we would class each as a form of exploitable property and how it could be exploited. When we consider the owning class, we need to separate ownership of those elements of property which function to provide shelter, work and food for ourselves and our communities from those used to exploit the same need in others. For example, owning a property that you live in is not in itself a definition of class, however owning a property that others live in and on which rents are charged – or which stands empty while others go without – *is* such a definition. While much property may not be fully owned by those identified as the named owners, what such ownership often provides is a source of capital to which further loans can be linked. In certain economic systems, the owner is allowed to both claim that they own nothing - thereby avoiding any taxes that may be owed - and to claim said ownership so that further loans can be generated in order to purchase further properties.

a) Ownership of accommodation

When we look at forms of accommodation, that is, the buildings that people are allowed to live in, we have two basic types: that which is used for the Individual's own living purposes; and that which is used owned to exploit the living requirements of others. When we then look at the *ownership* of such property, a complex mesh of ways by which the use of a property is paid for. In some cases, a property will be owned outright, while in others what is owned is a debt in the form of a mortgage that is paid off against the value of the property. Then we have the distinction between freehold and leasehold, where the former involves the ownership of both the building and the land on which it sits, while the latter involves the ownership of the bricks and mortar only and where the owner of the leasehold may also be required to pay a sum for the 'use' of the land on which the property stands. Finally, we have rental properties, where a tenant pays a sum in order to use the property as their home[20].

Where an Individual owns a property that is used for their own living purposes - and that of their Individual Unit - we would not normally regard this as an exploitable property. Such property is being used to provide the owner with a roof over their head and as such forms an essential part of their existence. Where an Individual owns property in addition to that which is used as their own living accommodation, this then becomes exploitable property. If an Individual owns further properties, these cannot be regarded as non-exploitable property, even if the Individual is the only person that ever uses them as residences. The reason for this is that, with the rise of 'second home' ownership, what has happened is that in many areas this has restricted the available housing stock, thereby artificially inflating prices for both homes for sale and for rent. In this

---

[20] Within the category of rental properties, we also have those which are sub-let, that is, where one person rents out the property from the owner and then rents it out to a third.

132

category, ownership of exploitable living accommodation, that is, property other than that which is used for their own living purposes, irrespective of whether or not it is actually being exploited, will place the Individual within the Owning Class.

b) Ownership of employment

Within the modern capitalist society, there is no longer what we would call 'free land' that is open for use by anyone and which an Individual might be able to use to make even a partial living for themselves. Instead, we have a system of ownership of all available resources, whereby the Individual has the 'choice' of working for themselves or working for someone else. Such a distinction, however, is the kind of over-simplification that is used to make it seem that everyone is in the position to set up on their own and make their fortune. What the lie belies is the sheer weight of demands that such a leap requires. In addition to having a recognised skill that others would be willing to pay for, the Individual would also be required to have all of the relevant skills required to run a business, access to sufficient finances to support themselves until their business develops, and the ability to promote whatever it is they are offering.

What this means is that, for most of us, we are reliant on someone else running a business that requires such skills as we are able to offer. So far, everything seems fine. However, what we need to remember is that, under capitalism, any potential employer will either be seeking to maximise their profits in order to increase their income or minimise their costs in order to make their service more cost effective. In either case, the key area in which overheads can be reduced is through the wages that are paid to any employees. As a consequence, any employee will always be paid less than the value of their labour.

Through the ownership of opportunities for employment, it is therefore possible to exploit the needs of others for gainful employment in order to generate wealth from their labour. By owning such property, the Individual is able to exercise control over the income of others. With those organisations that work on a 'non-profit' basis - such as the NHS, the civil service, the education system etc. - the concept of 'market forces' that are presumed to govern our economic system are used to drive down wages and ensure that employees are not paid according to their true value.

Within many organisations, we also have the development of exploitative practices where employees are 'encouraged' to work above and beyond what they are being paid for. Examples of this include unpaid overtime, unpaid internships, and the expectation that staff will be available at all times above and beyond their contracted hours. Such demands on the Individual are all forms of control placed upon their lives by those that own property related to employment.

(c) Ownership of utilities

In the modern capitalist society, we would identify all of those organisations that provide energy, public transport, water and waste removal, healthcare and finance as 'utilities'. Effectively, these are any organisations that function to provide the basic systems of social infrastructure that enable people to exist and for which they would not usually have the skills or facilities to provide for themselves. While there is an argument that housing and food should be included within this group, to some extent the Individual has a choice over where they live and where they get their food. With the utility services, where a person lives will determine which utility providers they can use. While the idea behind capitalism is that it will naturally create a system of competition between service providers, what we effectively get is a system of monopolies that are not governed by the 'rules' of the capitalist market and where ownership can be exploited to ensure massive payouts can be made to their shareholders. We would also add ownership within the financial sector of banks, loan companies and building societies to this. While, once again, we have a system whereby an Individual can choose from a large number of banks and financial service providers, all of these are effectively controlled by a collective self-interest, and whilst they will always deny this to be the case, the services that they provide are all remarkably similar.

Similar distinctions must be made for those aspects of property that have been sold by governments in order to provide investment in controlled utilities that have otherwise been denied by that government [21].   Such sell-offs of what is ostensibly public property promise financial gain for participants and provide them with the possibility of engagement in the machinery of social control, but its primary purpose is to cover up the history of under-funding. Such shares as are sold off rarely stay in public hands long as larger organisations - with considerably more financial backing than the ordinary member of society can muster - gain overall control. Controlling shares of these utilities are then transferred beyond the reach of ordinary members of the public.

(d) Ownership of ideas

The ownership of ideas began with the identification of certain forms of creation by an Individual to be covered by the legal framework of copyright and patent. In most cases, we would see this as an acceptable feature of the creation of an idea. For example, a musician who writes a song would get paid when the song is played on the radio because the

---

[21] In this model of class, 'government' does not refer to separate periods during which one party or another remains in power but refers to the entire period during which that system has existed. Parties and politicians come and go but the system of control remains the same.

radio station is exploiting the musician's work for their own commercial purposes. Similarly, an inventor who creates a new method for allowing a pen to release ink more evenly and with less mess - as Lazlo Biro did with the pen now commonly known as a 'biro' - has created something that benefits those who struggle to use fountain pens and, as such, he could control who can exploit his invention.

The problem that many will have with the laws of copyright and patent is that, while the compositions of a songwriter are not individually necessary to someone's day-to-day existence, once we get into the realms of safety-related inventions and medicines, the application of such laws, while protecting the rights of the creator, can have a negative impact on those requiring access to them. For example, with the creation of a new and essential medicine, a company can have a guaranteed monopoly on production of the medicine and can therefore charge whatever price they choose, ensuring that such medicines become the preserve of only the wealthiest nations. It is not always the case that such essential creations will be exploited in this way. For example, the Swedish inventors of the three-point seat belt realised that it was such as essential piece of car safety that they made the invention available to the whole motor industry[22].

---

[22] The modern form of the 3-point seat belt was invented by Nils Brohlin for Volvo, who made the invention "open patent" to allow all car manufacturers to use it in their vehicles.

(e) Ownership of roles

In some employment roles, an Individual is given the power to control the lives of others within their community. Such roles are usually qualified as part of the managerial roles that any organisation will have where an Individual or group of Individuals is tasked with identifying those that the organisation will employ etc. In most cases, we would see this as a necessary part of any organisation. Without such roles, it would be necessary to divert others from their usual roles, with the added issue that there is a greater duplication of tasks across multiple departments and higher costs. However, it should also be noted that some Individuals who occupy such managerial roles lack the required skills to carry out the task of managing others to any degree of effectiveness while others take the opportunity to exploit the power that it gives them to abuse those that they manage. Thus, the ownership of such roles, holding the unchecked power over others, must be included within our definition of those forms of ownership that place the holder of the role within the Owning Class.

3.5.3 The Political Purpose of the Owning Class

If we were to identify a single political purpose of the Owning Class, then it would be a stabilising force within society. This is not to say that they exist as a means to provide a benefit to those within the Working Class and Underclass but that what they provide is a multi-faceted buffer between those at the bottom-end of society and those that have control over them. If we look at the history of societies prior to the current form of capitalism, what we see are those where there is a great deal of discontent amongst the poorest on society, a continuing threat of open rebellion and, in some countries, actual revolution. What the Owning Class does is to provide a mechanism by which the economic system can be seen to 'succeed', deflecting discontent away from those with the most to a much more disparate group who sit at a closer relationship to the poorest; and who can be easily blamed for any of the ills of a society's failings. For example, if we look at what followed the Grenfell fire, what we see is a constant attempt for various bodies - local councils, building owners, cladding manufacturers etc - to deflect blame on to one of the other parties involved, leading to a long protracted hearing that never reached a point where the survivors and the families of those who had died could feel that justice had been served. What was very rarely held in question was the system that says that the cheapest option being offered is always good, that the first priority of any business is profit and that the impact on any Individual is of secondary consequence.

If we look at the capitalist economic systems employed across the world - whether it is in the *laisssez faire* economics of neo-liberal states such as the USA or the UK, or the state capitalist system that became the economic driving force in the Soviet Union, what we see most often is a very small coterie of people taking ownership of most of a nation's wealth, the bulk of the population 'getting by' and a sizeable chunk of society existing in poverty. If you study capitalist economic theory in any depth, this shouldn't happen. The 'market' is believed to provide both the means by which people can exist in society, and the balance that prevents them from having their needs exploited by businesses. As an employee, an Individual can always move on to one of their employers competitors willing to pay more for their services, and as a consumer there should always be a business willing to undercut the others in the provision of their services. Only someone deeply ingrained in this economic system will continue to believe that this is how the capitalist market actually works. If capitalism's market wasn't already a failed economic system, governments wouldn't need to consistently alter and revise budgets, bail out bankrupt banks and plough money into utilities in order to allow them to keep passing on huge sums to their shareholders.

So, if capitalism is such a failure, why haven't the poorest in society got rid of it already? Leaving aside the legal mechanisms that are designed to prop up a society's economic system, what we have is the Owning Class: a group of people who appear to have made it rich. The Owning Class are held up as proof that the system works. All the while that our attention can be directed towards someone who started with nothing and now runs a successful business, towards those who - by comparison to the poorest - we would consider to be wealthy - we can be distracted from looking at those that the system fails, those that lead a subsistence existence at best, that are reduced to begging, that die of hypothermia in unheated accommodation or die from malnutrition. These people are not a casual side-effect of this economic system but a necessary part of it. Wealth, as with all resources, is finite and when one small group of Individuals is guaranteed ownership of 99% of it, somebody else will have to go without. The Owning Class provide the barrier that stop us from focusing on this disparity. Each time we hand some loose change to someone living on the streets and consider the fact that our economic system has let them down, the couple on the telly buying their fifth rental property tells us that the system is working just fine.

And what better way to deflect any discontent that may arise than to have someone close at hand to blame. As a consequence, rather than pointing the finger at those who control society for failing to develop a system that actually works for the benefit of everyone, when interest rates rise and mortgage costs go up, we blame the landlords, the bank managers, the building societies. They are the ones that are causing us all of our financial problems. We may occasionally blame our elected politicians and vote for someone else, but it is extremely rare for them to ever be held either financially or criminally accountable for anything that they might have done to cause misery in someone's life.

3.5.4 Identifying Features of the Owning Class

The key factor in defining an Individual as a member of the Owning Class is that they will own property that allows for the exploitation of the basic needs of other Individuals and that such property is additional to that required for meeting their own basic needs. This can be broken down as follows:

1) That they will own property which allows for the exploitation of other Individuals' basic needs, including access to accommodation, employment and necessary utilities;

2) That such exploitable property may include the control of abstract properties through legislation in relation to copyright that allows them to exploit the needs of others in relation to their basic health and well-being requirements;

3) That such exploitable property may include control over the financial needs of other Individuals;

4) That such exploitable property may include the holding of a position that facilitates control over another Individual's employment and, therefore, their capacity to earn a living;

5) That in addition to the ownership of exploitable property, the Individual is not in a position to exercise

wider Societal Control which would place them within the Controlling Class.

3.6 THE CONTROLLING CLASS

Class has always been presented as something easy to define and immediately visible: we like our working classes in their 'blue collars' and cloth caps, with voices full of dropped vowels, regional accents and bad grammar; we like them to be roughly-hewn from the salt of the earth, un- or under-educated, preferably to the point of illiteracy, and confined to their own sections of society. Likewise, we prefer our upper classes to be easy to spot, but not for many years have our toffs dallied through the streets of Mayfair and Piccadilly, cane in hand and jaunty top hat doffing politely at the promenading ladies in St. James Park. In fact, the modern equivalent of the upper class in British society, the Controlling Class, have – despite the ostentatious show of wealth displayed by some – sought to disappear into the general morass of society's everyday mechanisms, successfully cloaking much of their wealth and the bulk of their influence and power. There is good reason for such disguise and subterfuge. When we consider that the majority of the world's wealth is owned by only 1% of its population, there would be considerable cause for that remaining 99% to relieve them of the heavy burden of affluence, as happened during the French Revolution, so the ability to wield Societal Control, and to have access to everything that this

144

can offer in modern Britain, needs to appear as a normal element of everyone's life; as the natural results of capitalism and 'democracy'. It is always much easier to control a large population if being controlled is fully accepted by the majority of these people. As such, the Controlling Class maintains a low profile wherever it can in order to avoid the conflict that would arise between the haves and the have nots so that only the bravura of royalty, footballers and film stars remains on view – a glimpse of possible wealth without the suggestion of them having control over our daily lives. But controlled we are.

So, without the commonly known pointers of top hat and tails, how are we to recognise the Controlling Class? It is no longer a matter of looking for the gimmicks of grandeur but of looking at the actual mechanisms of power within a society - who controls those mechanisms, who has access to those forms of control, by whatever means that may be. When we look closely, those we find in the Controlling Class are those who are able to use their wealth or their position of influence and power to control the lives of others across the whole of society. While the Owning Class may have the ability to control elements of the lives of Individuals or small groups, raising rents, back-tracking on pay-rises and such, the Controlling Class are able to exercise these same powers over wider aspects of society, both in the scope of their coverage of an the impact on the Individual's life, and in the number of people affected. The initial reaction to such an idea is that we are encountering what many will call a 'conspiracy theory'. We are convinced, fairly easily, that there are no shady meetings in the corridors of government where deals are made to control our very existence. Such an idea seems preposterous: Surely we control our own lives, make our own choices as to the path we tread?

What our disbelief masks is the reality of our situation. There may be no clearly defined conspiracies but decisions affecting the way we live our lives, the choices we are able to make, and the control we have over our own existence, all fall in the hands of others. We don't have control over the taxes that are demanded by government and much less over the way that the government spends the money it gets. The average Individual has little to no contact with their parliamentary representatives, will only encounter civil servants if they are pulled before televised parliamentary committees and they do not earn the level of income that would give then access to political lobbyists.

3.6.1 Summary of Class Composition

While our governments may wish to persuade us that, through the mechanics of representative democracy, all of us have a say in society with a substantial stake in Societal

146

Control and that consequently all of us should be seen as members of the Controlling Class, what we actually see is a distinct separation between those members of society that sit in positions of power and wealth - monarchs, politicians, billionaires, press barons etc. - and those who survive from one paycheck to the next, struggling to pay the bills, trying to save towards those 'little luxuries' like holidays, and hoping they can put enough by to leave something for their children. What we have is not so clear cut, however, for as well as those who are most visible to the public eye, we also find a number of others who can either exercise control over society or influence those that hold such control. In addition to these, we also have those who enforce that control. As a consequence, we must divide this group into three main segments:

(i) those who can wield direct control;
(ii) those who can influence those who wield direct control; and
(iii) those who enforce the control that others are able to wield.

The first group would include all of those who hold positions where they are able to pass laws or rulings, or enact societal decisions, while the second group would be those who have such close contact with the first group that they are able to apply pressure on those so that their own agenda can be fully met. Due to the nature of the political system employed in Britain, we would exclude those within the Working Class and Underclass from this group. Our politicians may wish to argue that the democratic process gives everyone 'direct influence'. However, having a vote once every four years and the chance to talk to an elected MP at a semi-regular surgery[23] cannot be treated as that Individual having such a level of influence.

(i) Direct Control

Those with direct access to societal control would include all those whose position gives them the ability to either make, or influence the making of, the rules by which society functions. This would include all politicians, whether elected or appointed and regardless of whether they are cabinet ministers, part of the government party in power or a serving MP for any other party with a seat in government. In addition to those who hold such positions at a national level, we would also include those who sit in similar positions at a county, metropolitan or borough level. We would also include those party members and staff who are in a position to have a direct say in the development and application of the policies of their particular party. The group would also include all of those senior civil servants with close working relationships with politicians who will take a key role in directing policy decisions. Those who work on the drafting of new laws alongside politicians, or

---

[23] Only some MPs offer surgeries to their constituents.

on the interpretation of existing laws, would also form part of this group.

We should then extend this group to those outside of the immediate political groupings to those who form part of the network of direct influence that politicians utilise, and are utilised by, or who are able to use their position to push their own agenda on wider society. The first group that would be included is the monarchy, as not only do we have a political system that is historically entwined with the role of the monarch through such events as the 'opening of parliament' but also through the fact that all laws require the consent of the monarch. While this may be regarded by many as little more than a long-standing tradition, what the royal family gain is direct access to most politicians, regular updates from senior politicians and civil servants on political trends, and the chance to intervene and have their own input on any laws that a government may want to propose.

Similarly, we have that same level of access to the political mechanisms of Britain being available to many of the similarly wealthy members of British society. This would include those various billionaires who have made their fortunes, those who would have been called 'press barons' in the last century but who now own many other forms of media as well. Due to the ability of our mainstream media to make or break a government, there is an argument to be made that the likes of the Murdoch family have a greater level of Societal Control within Britain than any politician could hope to have. Accordingly, the main representatives within all aspects of the mainstream media would also be included in this class as it is they that act as the established voice of authority[24]. We expect the version of events presented in the news, on current affairs programmes, in the newspapers, to be fair and unbiased and as such, with greater familiarity, we begin to trust implicitly what we are told without question. As a consequence, these Individuals are in a position not just to influence our behaviour but to manipulate it to suit their own agenda and that of those with whom they associate[25].

ii. Indirect Control

Those with Indirect Control fall into one of three groups: those who are able to apply influence on those with Direct Control, despite holding no such position themselves; those who are able to have tangential influence on those with Direct Control; and those whose role it is to ensure that the position of those with Direct Control is maintained.

---

[24] Regardless of which channel they appear on, the many news and current affairs programmes available are little more than variations on a theme.

[25] In most cases, such people are representing either their own aims for greater access to the established version of Societal Control or a section of those who already hold this, as the aim of the mainstream media has always been to ensure that the established order is maintained.

150

(a) Direct Influence

Those in a position of Direct Influence will include those whose chief role sits outside of the main law-making forums of a society, who are often unknown to the majority of society, but who are able to use their position to either by-pass a society's legal structures, or can use that position to gain easy access to those in higher levels of government. This would include those who are able to claim a private audience with the Prime Minister or the Chancellor on a regular basis as part of their role within society, such as the governor of the Bank of England, leaders of foreign governments, and CEOs of major companies. We would also include the major donors to political parties within this group, especially since so many of these seem to be granted particular benefits as a result of their donations, such as being gifted a lucrative seat in the House of Lords.

One of the main driving factors within this group, in addition to holding senior positions within private companies, seems to be wealth. While the British government is always being portrayed as the "mother of all democracies", the fact that having an excess of spare cash to hand out to politicians seems to be a major factor in who gets to decide what government actually does. A clear example of this would be the numerous millions that were given to wealthy friends of the Conservative government during the COVID crisis to provide equipment to the NHS -

something which most had no experience of and much of which never appeared,

(b) Tangential Influence

To continue with the COVID link in terms of those having connections with those in power, one clear example of those having tangential influence would be the landlord of the pub where Secretary of Health Matt Hancock drank who was given a very lucrative contract to provide PPE to the NHS, despite having no experience in anything similar, and simply because he was the landlord of an MP's local. Within the Controlling Class, then, we find those with close connections to government – both as elected officials or within the higher echelons of the civil service - who would best be describe as "friends and acquaintances". This would also include numerous members of extended family. Anyone, it seems, with the right connections can become a millionaire overnight courtesy of the right government minister. While such people within this group may not appear to have any level of control beyond the Personal, they are able to use personal relationships to their own benefit.

(c) Agents of Control

Finally, we have what can be best described as the 'agents of control': those who are given legal powers to enforce the rules imposed upon the rest of society, such as the police, the judiciary, the army and such civil enforcers as bailiffs. While this group may be comprised of those who would – in any other profession – be considered to be members of the Working Class due to their reliance on the fruits of their labour for what little control they may have over their own existence, they have made the active choice to undertake roles that enable them to exercise greater power over other members of society. There are a large number of people within any modern society who, while ostensibly having no control above the level of Personal Control, must be included within the scope of the Controlling Class due to the roles they chose to undertake. They must be classed as members of the Controlling Class not because they are *in* positions of Societal Control, but because they act as the *agents* of such control. The obvious role included within this would be that of a society's security forces. In Britain, in addition to the various county and metropolitan police forces, it would also include those government agencies that participate in the monitoring of citizens activities that may not fit with the prevailing ideology, such as MI5 and sections of the departments of the Home Office and the Foreign Office.

In some instances, while the armed forces of a society will be predominantly employed to engage in overseas conflict, there are many instances where they will be used within roles that support the requirements of the Controlling Class against other citizens. An historical example of this would be the formation of armies by both Royalists and

Parliamentarians during the English Civil War, where members of the Working Class were conscripted by both sides and forced to fight against their own, in many cases with brothers fighting each other and fathers fighting their sons. A more recent example would be use of the army during the miner's strike of 1984, where the British government bolstered the numbers of police present at various picket lines with squaddies from barracks up and down the country, dressed in full police uniform but without the identifying insignia that all police officers are required to wear when on Duty. In such cases, those involved would be classed as members of the Controlling Class because of their participation in activities whose sole purpose is to undermine the Working Class and to ensure that desires of the Controlling Class continue to be met.

While some who are employed at the most senior levels within these services will have direct access to, for example, politicians, the majority will have no such contacts but rather will be in a position where the work that they undertake relates to either the enforcement of society's laws, many of which are written to ensure that the Controlling Class retains their position and wealth, or to the enforcement of the *desires* of the Controlling Class. In the latter case, such work may not necessarily be legal, moral or even remotely honest. They may not be able to access those who do wield control but they have chosen to undertake a position within society that allows them to effectively become a tool of Societal Control.

3.6.2 The Political Purpose of the Controlling Class

At its most basic, the Controlling Class is that which wields power to control the rest of society. While this may not seem innocuous in any way, since someone needs to be there take the important decisions, what happens in modern capitalist societies is that such a class becomes the centre for all wealth and power within a society. While we may think that our lives come entirely under our own control, the *actual* control that we are able to hold is very different from our *perception.* Our taxes – and consequently our available income – are decided elsewhere; someone else defines the amount we pay in rents[26]; mortgage rates are controlled by the finance industry; our access to benefits comes under constant scrutiny and review by government agencies.

Where Societal Control does not fall within the full reach of those who hold Personal and Dependent control, those who wield Societal Control will rarely use it for the benefit of society. The reason for this is that such power creates not just the possibility of the exploitation of some property but

---

[26] Rents are always portrayed as being 'market driven', however, through such tactics as limiting the building of social housing, holding properties empty, this market can be artificially inflated to the detriment of the tenant.

of all society. As a consequence, the impact of the access to all that can be gained from society - the accumulation of wealth, the establishment of contacts so that control can always be accessed etc. - means that the Individual becomes inherently corrupted by their access to power.

3.6.3 Identifying Features of the Controlling Class

The Controlling Class can be defined by the following criteria:

1) They are able to exercise Societal Control, that is, they are able to extend the limits of their power beyond both their own Individual Unit and those who have Communal Control.

2) The role or position held within society enables them to make or influence decisions made within government, industry, the legal sector or the banking sector, where such decisions will affect the larger portion of society either at a local or national level.

3) They are in a position whereby they have easy contact with those who hold direct Societal Control and as such are able to influence decision-making to suit their own requirements.

4) They are able to act as the agents of the Controlling Class, ensuring that any decisions taken by them are imposed on the rest of society, irrespective of whether there is a moral justification for such.

4) Their role is given the power to exercise and enforce laws over the rest of society, allowing for the application of arbitrary enforcement.

BRIEF CONCLUSIONS

Conclusions

Through the use of the Control System for the analysis of class, it is possible to create class definitions for any society as it allows us to determine a standard degree to which the Individuals in society can be easily measured in terms of their ability to take control over their lives. What the four key Circles of Control give us is a set of measures which can be applied to any society without having to adjust for the historical period, the economic system or any political bias. Such a system allows for this analysis to be applied against any society from the simplest inter-family units of the prehistoric period all the way through to those societies where the population stretches into billions of Individuals, such as modern China.

4.1 The Control Model

The use of a simple model that looks at the basis of how a society functions, what control people have over their own lives, whether anyone in turn has control over them and what happens to those people who become dependent on a society, it is possible to then look at the way that any class system will work. The Control Model allows us to do just this. It is not dependent on a particular social structure or economic system being in place, it does not require any particular set of circumstances and as such it can be used to assess any form of society, from the simplest unit though to complex empires. What this allows us to do is work out what freedoms we should expect an Individual to have within any given society, what level of external control is placed upon them and what are the defining features of those that sit within each Circle of Control.

By applying the Control Model to modern Britain, what we see is a deeply entrenched stratification within the social structure with a clear differentiation between the four Circles of Control that we use to define class. While there is some overlap - for example between those that occupy the Dependent Circle with those that occupy the Personal Circle of Control, there is a clear distinction between each. What we see is a society where the Circles of Control are firmly separated, so that the majority of the population will have no access to the Circle of Societal Control. We begin at the Dependent and then move out through the remaining Circles of Control, with the bulk of the population sitting within the Circle of Personal Control and with fewer Individuals able to access control at a Communal Level and fewer still at a Societal Level.

4.1 Class Structure

Once this inequality in society has been identified, we can then look at what this analysis presents us within a Class-based analysis. In British society, with the definite separation between the different Circles of Control, we are not looking at a society where there is an equality of access to control at all levels. We have those who have limited access to any form of control and in addition to those who occupy this position through what we might call the 'nature of existence' - such as old age, illness or infirmity - we also have those who are made dependent through the forces placed upon them - such as low pay, discrimination, or abuses of power. Such a society, therefore, is also not going to give us a class system that reflects an equality of access to control.

Instead, we have a clearly defined class structure, with a small section of society holding sway, and three further sections, each holding less and less power to control their lives, with those who have Dependent Control occupying the lowest level. As stated in the first section, this structure does not flow seamlessly from bottom to top, and there is no class ladder by which an Individual can climb up 'through the ranks'. What we have is those who have control just at the Dependent Level sitting within an Underclass at the bottom of society, closely tied to, but also distinctly separate from, the Working Class, which comprises those who hold a limited degree of Personal Control as a result of the work that they undertake. Due to the precarious hold on control that many of the Working Class have, there is a great deal of overlap between the two. As a consequence, these two classes sit together. At this point, we have a clear break within the class system which results from the economics of property ownership. While extended levels of ownership across the wider society should facilitate greater levels of equality, the economic system is so manipulated that ownership at this level only supports the Individual in the acquisition of property where it facilitates the exploitation of the needs of other Individuals/Individual Units. There is no blurring between the Working Class and the Owning Class, as the Working Class-Middle Class format of class systems generates. The Individual either owns exploitable property or does not own exploitable property.

It is at this point where were we find a second overlap between classes which results from the accrual of wealth and the access that an excess of this would give to those who hold power within the Circle of Societal Control. Those within the Controlling Class apply control for their own benefit first and foremost. Even the most ardent supporter of the Working Class within parliament will first apply their power to support their own personal agenda. This is not necessarily a criticism, since any Individual will service the needs of their own Individual

Unit before that of others. However, what we see within successive governments is the use of power by Individuals to support the desires (not needs) of those that they most closely associate with, that is, with other members of the Controlling Class. What this means is the misuse of state legal systems to ensure that the wealth of their class is not threatened. In practice, this is the Controlling Class using their power to accrue more and more property for the sole purpose of exploiting others.

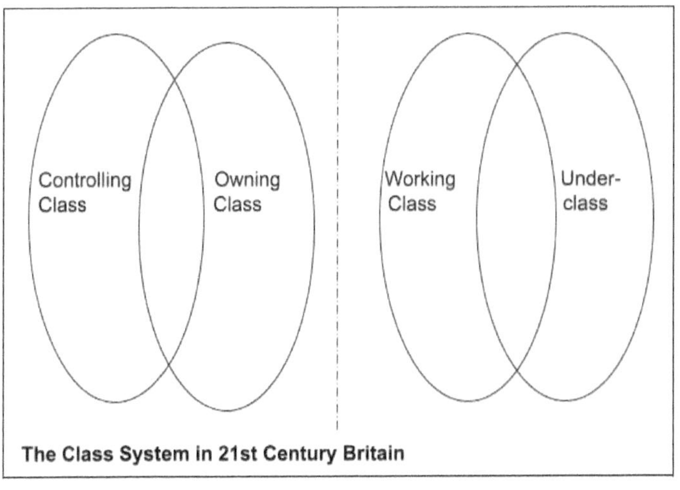

Fig. 11: The Class System in 21st Century Britain

What we have, therefore, is a class system with two very distinct sections: we have the Underclass and the Working Class on one side and the Owning and

Controlling Class on the other side. There is no clear link between the two, since there is very limited capacity for anyone within the first section to move into the second without first having access to either excess wealth that would allow them to buy their way into the Owning Class, or the friends and connections to have access to those within the Controlling Class.

4.2 Class Mobility

We like to think of those at the top of society as those with all the wealth, all the property, all the power. We think immediately of politicians, statesmen, kings and queens, the directors of multinational companies. We think of the grand luxury in which their lives exist and, understandably, we feel the pangs of jealousy. These are distractions, designed to guide our sight towards the opulence, the glamorous lifestyle, the importance. We are lured towards aspirations of a better life for ourselves, ensuring that we compare these states of being to those in which we find ourselves. We look at our own lives and see, by comparison, the paucity of our being: we have nothing, they have everything. In seeing this, we are guided towards the notion that there is a viable progression from one to the other – we may be poor, but one day we can be rich. The façade of wealth and opulence that we see when we look at

166

those at the top of society is there to conceal the true nature of this class' role within society: Control.

In traditional models of class, it is possible to rise through the ranks and transcend the financial poverty at the bottom. What the application of the Control Model shows when we analyse British society is that such levels of mobility are essentially non-existent. While transition between the Working Class and the Underclass is fairly fluid, this is usually a result of their treatment by those in the Owning and Controlling Classes, both of which are effectively closed off to the majority of society. For most members of the Underclass, transition to the Working Class is achieved only through gaining a position of employment, thereby increasing the level of income and removing the need for financial support.

Where people's position within the Underclass is determined not by income but by prejudice, such transition is much harder to achieve. Their position is determined by factors entirely outside of their control: while they may be able to get better jobs or raise their income, they cannot control the way that the Controlling Class presents them as the enemy of the rest of the Working Class. Once an Individual has been stigmatised within society, the accompanying prejudice is unlikely to disappear within their lifetime.

Transition beyond the Working Class to a point where a point where they can begin to establish Communal Control and join the Owning Class is highly difficult as it is limited to just two options:

> 1) Promotion into a position where an Individual gains ownership of employment; or
> 2) Accumulation of sufficient disposable income to provide capital with which property above and beyond Individual requirements can be obtained.

For the majority of those within the Working Class, such transition is unlikely. In addition, within British society, the idea that an Individual or group of Individuals can attain a collective, communal control whereby equality across all is established is impossible.

4.3 Women and Class

So far, what has been covered in terms of defining the class structure within Britain is class in its most general sense, where the Individual has been identified in terms that assume an equality of existence between all Individuals within the same class or within the same Individual Unit. What has not been so clearly defined is the impact that the manner in which women are treated within society has upon their class position. When we consider that, throughout all levels of class in the UK, women's pay is, on average, 8.3% lower than men's, we must acknowledge that their ability to control their existence at the Personal level will be less than that of many of their male counterparts.

While there will always be women who are able to wield societal control without any men in positions equal to, or above them – Queen Elizabeth II and Margaret Thatcher being the prime examples in recent history – for most women, in whatever role they fulfill, they will find themselves compared less favourably to men. An example of this difference can be seen in a comparison of the treatment of Boris Johnson and Liz Truss during their tenures as Prime Minister by both their peers and the national media. While it would be fair to say that neither was able to display the intellectual skills required to undertake such a role, Johnson was able to inflict levels of financial mismanagement, corruption and democide over a prolonged period while retaining massive support from both his fellow MPs and the national media. Truss, on the other hand, lasted only a matter of weeks before being forced to resign from the post. While she had crashed the economy - but not to the extent that it couldn't recover - her predecessor had been responsible for over 200,000 deaths through his sheer incompetence. In addition to demonstrating the true meagreness of parliamentary morality, placing money so far above human life, it further reinforces the misogynistic treatment of women within British society.

What this level of discrimination contributes to is a situation where Working Class women are more likely to be found within the Underclass than a man fulfilling a similar role within society or from within the same Individual Unit. Even in the Controlling and Owning Class, the impact of such discrimination will be felt and while this may not cause a change in the person's social class, it will cause them to have to work much harder to achieve the same results. As a consequence, women are likely to wield far less control than their male counterparts regardless of the class they fall within. However, when we come to look at women within the Working Class, the discrepancies in financial well-being, combined with both state-initiated and 'cultural' misogyny, are likely to lead to far more women falling within the Underclass.

Also by Alfie Cooke

Art
Fragments of a Memory: The Art of Annie Poulter (2014)

Fiction
The Disposable Actions of a Purgatory Love (2014)
Filaments of Chaos (2014)
Learning Goat (2017)
Babylon Arcades (2022)
Valium Drag (2023)
Slag Heaping (2023)
Hide Me From The Dark That Seeks To Find Me (2024)

Music
Beginning Free Improvisation (2014)
Music from Within a Rogue Nation (Bb, C, Eb) (2014)
Songbook Vol. 1 (Eb edition) (2014)
Symphony No. 1 (Blues Adagio) full score (2014)

Poetry
Death Rides A Wild Horse (1996)
The Grown Man Fell To His Knees And Wept Just Like
        A Baby (as Alfie Howard) (1997)
Unknown Languages (2023)
Like Screaming Blood and Deathly Wail (2024)

Politics
Class 2025 (2024)

Religion
The Ethics of Revolutionary Buddhism (2022)